Rules *of*
Engagement

Rules *of* Engagement

PREPARING FOR YOUR ROLE IN THE SPIRITUAL BATTLE

Derek Prince

Chosen

Grand Rapids, Michigan

© 2006 by Derek Prince Ministries–International

Published by Chosen Books
A division of Baker Publishing Group
P.O. Box 6287, Grand Rapids, MI 49516-6287
www.chosenbooks.com

Seventh printing, June 2007

Printed in the United States of America

Library of Congress Cataloging-in-Publication Data
Prince, Derek.
    Rules of engagement : preparing for your role in the spiritual battle / Derek Prince.
        p.   cm.
    Ministry letters, written 1993–2003.
    ISBN 10: 0-8007-9406-0 (pbk.)
    ISBN 978-0-8007-9406-4 (pbk.)
    1. Spiritual warfare—Biblical teaching. 2. Christian life—Biblical teaching. I. Title.
BS680.S73P77 2006
248.4—dc22   2005026675

Contents

Part 3 Battle in the Heavenlies

Part 4 Enduring to the End

Introduction

Derek Prince reached the zenith of his visibility and vigor well before the current era of the media ministry "star." Nevertheless he stands as one of the truly extraordinary Bible teachers and theologians of the twentieth century.

A British citizen born in India, Prince was Eton educated and Cambridge trained, a contemporary and acquaintance of C. S. Lewis. For a time prior to his dramatic conversion experience, he held a prestigious fellowship in ancient and modern philosophy at Cambridge. But once his amazing intellect was submitted to Christ and illuminated by the Holy Spirit, he became a formidable force for communicating the truths of Scripture. As a classically trained philosopher and unabashed charismatic, he was that too-rare confluence of academic rigor and openness to the supernatural. The Word and power. Truth and Spirit.

Across the better part of nearly six decades, in countless cities on six continents, Derek Prince taught, preached, encouraged, proclaimed, imparted and inspired. And all along the way, he wrote. It would be difficult to overstate the impact and influence this humble, self-effacing teacher has had around the world.

In the autumn of 2003, Derek Prince died in his beloved Jerusalem, his home for nearly twenty years. He was 88. He left behind some wonderful gifts. To those who had the privilege of knowing him, he left an inspiring example—one of yieldedness to God, love for the Church, a heart for Israel and a roaring passion to see God's people walk in the fullness of the freedom and authority Christ purchased for them. To all of us he left an astonishing volume of teaching in books, articles, sermons and letters.

You now hold in your hands a unique fragment of that treasure. Between 1993 and 2003, Derek generated scores of "teaching letters" written expressly for his friends and partners in ministry. These ministry letters represent some of the deepest and richest teaching you will find on important but neglected topics such as personal character, true worship and the power of the Word of God. It is our pleasure to present some of the finest of these in this collection.

It is especially appropriate that we do so because, on more than one occasion, Derek expressed his strong desire that his ministry continue beyond his homegoing. Few things meant more to him than the knowledge that the truths he spent his life proclaiming would continue to be proclaimed to the saints.

In life he poured himself out to see God's people grow to maturity in the Word. May this collection be an extension of that legacy in your life.

The editors of Chosen Books

Part 1

Building a Soldier's Character

1

Our Struggle with Obedience

The Spirit of the Lord is moving to and fro throughout the whole earth looking for a certain type of person— one whose heart is perfect toward God. Whenever the Holy Spirit finds such a soldier in the army, God delights to show Himself strong in his behalf, granting an open manifestation of His power and approval in that person's life and ministry. He is waiting to move openly in power and in blessing.

This kind of involvement in spiritual battles takes all a person has to give. The Bible tells us that Abraham was that kind of soldier. And Job. Scripture says that they had just such a heart. They accepted the challenges facing them and reached the climax of spiritual growth.

But wait! you say. *First things first. I am not Abraham or Job! How can I possibly have a heart that is perfect toward God?*

If that is what it takes to prepare for my role in spiritual battle, if the rules of engagement can only be embraced by one whose heart is perfect toward God, I might face defeat before I even start!

No, you are not Abraham, but you can accept a fresh challenge from God. And you are not Job, but you can have a right attitude toward God and a right attitude toward evil. You see, we will discover that there is no neutrality in perfection toward God. A soldier in His army does not compromise with anything that is unpleasing to Him; you must be absolutely committed to obedience—no matter what it costs. And be reminded, as every soldier knows, it does cost something to be approved of God!

We are all coming to the point of the consummation of the purpose of God for the ages. And the message of God for every person who is going to take his place in what God is doing is this: "Walk before Me and be perfect." This is how we will fulfill our roles in the spiritual battle—day-to-day trials *now* and greater battles *to come.*

For more than fifty years, I have tried to help people with innumerable problems in their lives. Eventually, I have come to a surprising conclusion: *Our basic problem as human beings is that we do not realize how valuable we are.* As we will discuss further in the next chapter, we need to focus more on the way God sees us than the way we see ourselves. We often miss the call to join in the great battle because we think that we cannot make the grade.

Consequently, we make the most tragic mistakes. We are like a person who is legally heir to a vast fortune, but we sell off our entire inheritance for something incomparably less valuable: a night of sex, a joint of marijuana, a drunken party, a crooked financial scheme.

Or we may value ourselves a little higher, perhaps seeking some prestigious position in politics or the entertainment world, or even some high ecclesiastical office. Yet for all its prestige, it does not compare with the value of our inheritance—which we give in exchange for it.

God wants to move in power in our lives. He wants us to move victoriously through the years ahead, learning more about Him and learning more about ourselves. Thus, we will cover a lot of ground as we take our places in the spiritual battle raging around us. We will learn how a soldier's character is developed and what to do when facing tests. We will enter the training camp of the greatest teacher and helper on earth—the Holy Spirit. Then we will move into battle in the heavenlies, learning many schemes of the enemy. And finally, we will take up our stations and put to the test the character that endures.

Our goal is to prepare. Let us start by going back briefly to the beginning of biblical history: first, to Adam, the ancestor of our race, and then to Jacob, a patriarch who epitomizes in many ways our struggle with obedience. It is in these ancient narratives that we find the age-old obstacle to taking up God's rules of engagement: It is *independence*.

Our Fallen Motivation

"You will be like God, knowing good and evil" (Genesis 3:5). Surely that is a lofty and commendable ideal—to be like God. How could there be anything wrong with that? Yet in the mouth of Satan—manifesting himself in the form of a serpent—it enticed Adam and Eve into a disaster, the evil consequences of which have affected all their descendants.

What was the undetected snare to which Adam and Eve fell prey? It was the *motive*—unstated, but implied—the promise of independence. Once you know good and evil, you will be free to make your own decisions. You will no longer be dependent on God. This self-asserting desire for independence has been transmitted by inheritance to the whole human race. It is the distinctive mark of the "old Adam"—the fallen sinful nature that lurks in each of us.

13

Historically, there have been various routes that humanity has followed in seeking independence from God. The first is *knowledge*. In the Garden of Eden there were two special trees—the tree of *life* and the tree of *knowledge*. It was a critical moment in history, when Adam and Eve turned away from the tree of life and chose the tree of knowledge.

Ever since, the attainment of knowledge has been one main goal of humanity. Over the last two or three centuries this has expressed itself in an ever-increasing emphasis on *science*. (Our English word *science* is directly derived from *scientia*, the Latin word for "knowledge.")

This explosion of science has not, however, solved humanity's most basic problems: injustice, cruelty, war, poverty, disease. In fact, in some ways, it has increased them. Science has provided man with weapons of mass destruction that could obliterate the entire human race and turn the whole earth into a desolate waste. Furthermore, some of these weapons are in the hands of cruel and wicked men who would not be deterred from using them by any considerations of mercy or morality.

A second route that humanity has followed in seeking to achieve independence from God is at first surprising. It is *religion*. In various different forms men have established religious rules and systems of worship so complete and all-sufficient that there is no further need of God. All they have to do is to keep their rules.

This is true of some forms in which various of the world's major religions are practiced—Judaism, Islam, Buddhism and even some versions of Christianity. In all these religions people can become so satisfied with their rules and procedures that they become independent of God Himself. This explains why earnest, religious people are sometimes the slowest to respond to the Gospel's offer of grace that cannot be earned.

Yet another way that man seeks to achieve independence from God is by amassing large amounts of money and material possessions. Jesus told a parable of a rich landowner who became so successful that he had no more room to store his crops (see Luke 12:16–20). He decided to build even larger storage facilities and then he would say to his soul,

> "'Soul, you have many goods laid up for many years; take your ease; eat, drink, and be merry.' But God said to him, 'Fool! This night your soul will be required of you; then whose will those things be which you have provided?'"
>
> verses 19–20

Countless people throughout history have been lured by the same desire for independence into making the same tragic error. Countless people are still making it today.

This desire to be independent of God is the distinctive mark of all who belong to the kingdom of Satan—rebellious angels, demons, fallen humanity. It is also the distinctive mark of the "world," concerning which Jesus said of His disciples, "They are not of the world, just as I am not of the world" (John 17:16).

In this sense, the "world" consists of all the people who have never submitted themselves to the authority of God's appointed King—the Lord Jesus Christ. Some of these are moral, religious people, but when they are challenged with God's requirement of unreserved submission to the Lordship of Jesus, the rebellious, independent "old man" rises to the surface and they reject God's offer of salvation through grace alone.

Lonely, Alienated Humanity

This desire to be independent of God separates men from God's other creatures, who exhibit uniform, unquestioning dependence upon their Creator.

None of the heavenly bodies displays any desire for independence. "The moon marks off the seasons, and the sun knows when to go down" (Psalm 104:19, NIV). The stars answer to their names when God calls them. "He counts the number of the stars; He calls them all by name" (Psalm 147:4).

No matter how turbulent the elements may at times appear to be, they always obey their Creator—"Fire and hail, snow and clouds; stormy wind, fulfilling His word" (Psalm 148:8).

The same is true of the animal creation. "The young lions roar after their prey, and seek their food from God" (Psalm 104:21). "This great and wide sea, in which are innumerable teeming things, living things both small and great. . . . These all wait for You, that You may give them their food in due season" (Psalm 104:25, 27). Concerning the birds, Jesus tells us, "Your heavenly Father feeds them" (Matthew 6:26).

No wonder that rebellious man at times feels lonely and alienated from the universe around him, in which the other creatures all function together in dependence on their Creator.

The Way Back to Dependence

On the cross Jesus provided a double remedy for our fallen condition. First, He paid on our behalf the full penalty for all our sins, and thus made it possible for God to forgive our sins without compromising His own justice. Second, Jesus also identified Himself with the independent, self-seeking ego that dominates our fallen nature. In Jesus that rebel was put to death. "Our old man [the rebel] was crucified with Him" (Romans 6:6).

To become disciples of Jesus, we must each avail ourselves of this double remedy. First, we must make sure that—through repentance and faith—all our sins have been forgiven. Second, we must agree to the sentence of death pronounced upon our rebellious, independent ego.

Hence the conditions for discipleship that Jesus laid down: "So likewise, whoever of you does not forsake all that he has cannot be My disciple" (Luke 14:33).

The word translated "forsake" could be rendered "say farewell to." Becoming a disciple of Jesus means saying farewell to everything on which we would normally depend—family, friends, money, career, worldly honor or prestige. Once we have truly renounced all these things, God may return to us any of them that fit in with His purpose for our lives. But we are no longer possessors; we are merely stewards, required to give an account of the use we make of them. Our dependence becomes solely upon God.

Sometimes it may take a crisis—or even a seeming disaster—to bring us to the place where we fully acknowledge our dependence on God. I think of Paul's journey to Rome, described in Acts 27. God had a special plan for Paul to go to Rome, the capital of the Roman Empire. As the "apostle of the Gentiles," he had a unique contribution to make to the Church there.

Yet Paul traveled as a prisoner in chains. The ship he traveled on encountered a storm so terrific that for two weeks they never saw the sun by day or the stars by night. Finally they were all shipwrecked on the rugged coast of Malta. There—to cap it all—Paul was bitten by a poisonous snake (see Acts 27:13–28:6)! If it was God's will for Paul to go to Rome, why did he experience such extraordinary trials on his journey there?

As I pondered this, I recalled a phrase in Acts 27:20: "All hope that we would be saved was finally given up." That was the purpose of Paul's trials: to bring him to the place where *all hope was given up*. Now Paul had nothing left to hope in but God Himself. That was when he proved in experience that God is all-sufficient. God brings us to the place of total dependence upon Himself, to demonstrate that He is totally dependable.

Having come to this place of total dependence, Paul was ready for his ministry to the Christians in Rome. His journey there had prepared him. Emptied of all self-sufficiency, he was a yielded channel through which God's blessings could flow. We tend to forget that although Paul was an apostle, he was also still a disciple—under the Lord's discipline.

Gradually—through the years—I have been learning this lesson of total dependence. I have to confess that I have been a slow learner. God has used different circumstances at different times to enforce the lesson. But I have discovered that the more completely I depend on God, the more He surprises me by the results that follow—results that I could never have achieved as long as I depended on my own efforts.

Jacob's Surrender

Jacob is one character in the Bible who had a literal physical struggle to give up his independence. As a young man, he was astute, ambitious, self-seeking. He exploited a moment of physical weakness in his brother, Esau, to buy from him his birthright—as the elder son—for a bowl of soup. Then to obtain the paternal blessing (which normally went together with the birthright) he deceived his father, Isaac—who was blind—and passed himself off as Esau.

Yet neither the birthright nor the blessing did Jacob much good. To escape Esau's vengeance he fled to Mesopotamia and became a refugee with his uncle Laban. Here again he demonstrated his astuteness. He married Laban's two daughters and acquired most of Laban's wealth.

Then the Lord told him that it was time to return to the land of his inheritance. On his way back, however, he encountered a mysterious stranger who wrestled with him all night. Eventually the stranger dislocated Jacob's thigh (containing the strongest muscle in his body), and Jacob clung to him in helpless dependence. Only after that encounter could Jacob actually return to his inheritance. But for the rest of his life he walked with a limp—the outward mark of independence surrendered.

Who was the stranger that wrestled with Jacob? First, he is called a *Man* (see Genesis 32:24). But the next day Jacob said, "I have seen *God* face to face" (Genesis 32:30, emphasis added). Later the prophet Hosea said of this encounter: "Yes, he [Jacob] struggled with the *Angel*" (Hosea 12:4, emphasis added).

So this same Person was a Man, yet God, and also an Angel—that is, a messenger from God. There is only one Person in the universe who answers to this description: a Man, yet God, and also a messenger from God. It is the Person who was manifested in human history as Jesus of Nazareth—a Man, yet also God, and a messenger from God to man.

Jacob's destiny was finally settled by this encounter. After this, he was restored to his inheritance and was also reconciled with his brother, Esau.

Perhaps you feel that until now you have not been fully engaged. Your heart has been more like Adam's or Jacob's than, say, Abraham's or Job's. You, too, have been struggling in your own strength rather than letting God direct your life. If so, you need to do just what Jacob did: surrender yourself without reservation to the Lord Jesus Christ.

Would you like to settle this before we go further in our journey? Here, then, is a prayer you may pray:

Lord Jesus, I believe that You truly are my Savior and that You desire absolutely committed obedience. But I have not kept my heart "perfect" toward You. I have compromised by seeking my own path and relying on my own strength. I repent! I lay down my independence and I submit myself without reservation to Your Lordship. From now on I will depend on Your all-sufficient grace.

Ready? Let's move forward! The army is marching. But now comes the first test: One important character trait determines your readiness for battle. We discover it along with Gideon's army.

2

Who Will Qualify?

Recently, I have been strongly impressed by the words of the Lord in Isaiah 55:8–9:

> "For my thoughts are not your thoughts, neither are your ways my ways," declares the LORD. "As the heavens are higher than the earth, so are my ways higher than your ways and my thoughts than your thoughts."
>
> NIV

As I was pondering on the vast gap that separates God's ways and thoughts from ours, I was forcefully reminded of the account of Gideon and his army in Judges 6–8.

At this time, Israel had fallen into sin and idolatry and—as a judgment—God permitted vast hordes of Midianites to invade her land each year and rob her of her harvest.

One day, while Gideon was furtively threshing wheat in a winepress—to hide it from the Midianites—the Angel of the LORD appeared to him and said, "The LORD is with you, you mighty man of valor!" (Judges 6:12). Obviously the Lord saw Gideon quite differently from the way that he saw himself. Gideon saw himself as young, weak and ineffective. The Lord hailed him as a *mighty man of valor.*

As I mentioned earlier, we need to be less concerned with how we see ourselves and more concerned with how God sees us. In Christ, each one of us is a "new man . . . created according to God, in true righteousness and holiness" (Ephesians 4:24). Viewing ourselves like this will inevitably affect the way we engage in warfare.

The Lord commissioned Gideon to lead Israel in battle against the Midianites. In response, Gideon assembled an army by the well of Harod, with the Midianites encamped to the north.

What were the numbers on both sides?

Gideon's army:	32,000
Midianite army:	135,000

Thus, Gideon with 32,000 men (see Judges 7:3) faced 135,000 Midianites (see Judges 8:10). He was outnumbered more than four to one. So imagine Gideon's reaction when the Lord told him, "The people who are with you are too many" (Judges 7:2)!

The Lord instructed Gideon to send away all those in his army who were fearful and afraid. As a result, 22,000 men departed and Gideon was left with 10,000. At this point he was outnumbered more than thirteen to one.

But God was not finished! To Gideon's astonishment, He said, "The people are still too many" (verse 4).

Then He instructed Gideon to bring his men down to the water, so that He might test them there by the way they drank from the water. All those who went down on both knees to drink were eliminated. Only those who lapped like a dog passed the test (see Judges 7:4–7).

One Essential Character Requirement

The test focused on one single character requirement: *vigilance.*

Picture first those who drank in the normal way. Laying aside the shield from the left arm and the spear—or sword—from the right arm, they went down on both knees and buried their faces in the water. In this posture, they were totally vulnerable to a surprise attack. They could not see any approaching enemy, nor did they have their weapons ready to use. In the time it took to get themselves ready, the enemy would have overcome them.

What about those who lapped like dogs? When a dog drinks, it does not bury its nose in the water, it stretches out its tongue and laps the water up into its mouth, usually splashing some water around.

How, then, should we picture the men who lapped? Judges 7:6 says that, with a cupped hand, they scooped up the water to their mouths. In other words, they went down on one knee only. Retaining their shield on their left arm, with the right arm they set down their spear or sword beside them. In this posture, they remained alert, watching constantly for any surprise attack. Their shields were already in position and they could instantly pick up their spear or sword and have it ready to use. There was no possibility of the enemy catching them off-guard.

Only three hundred of Gideon's men passed this second test. They were facing 135,000 Midianites. They were outnumbered 450 to 1!

I can picture some of those who were dismissed saying to themselves, "Well, thank God we're out of that! That Gideon must be crazy. What difference does it make how a man drinks water? Let's see what will become of him and the idiots who stayed with him."

In the outcome, of course, Gideon and his three hundred engineered a surprise attack that threw the Midianites into total confusion. After that, other Israelites rallied behind Gideon and inflicted a total defeat on the Midianites.

The proportions are illuminating. Only three hundred men fulfilled the qualifications for the initial attack. But once they broke through, thousands of Israelites were eager to pursue the fleeing Midianites.

This whole account illustrates how different God's ways are from ours. Left to himself, Gideon would surely have concluded, "The people with me are too few. I need to get reinforcements." But God's perspective was exactly the opposite. *"The people with you are too many."* In the end, Gideon was left with less than one out of a hundred of those who originally joined him. For God, the question is not "How many people?" but "What kind of people?"

A Personal Assessment

In the light of this account, we each need to make a personal assessment. In the army that God is gathering today, would I be one of the few who qualify? Or would I be like the 22,000 who were eliminated because they gave way to fear? Or like the 9,700 who laid down their weapons and buried their faces in the water to drink?

It is easy—and often normal—to *bury our faces* in the business of daily living; to be absorbed in all the practical needs that confront us every day; to forget that we are in a spiritual conflict with unseen forces of darkness who are continually watching for an opportunity to catch us unprepared.

To maintain unceasing vigilance in every situation demands conscious, personal discipline. It goes beyond all our normal concepts of Christian conduct and morality. Yet the New Testament clearly warns us: "Be sober, *be vigilant*; because your adversary the devil walks about like a roaring lion, seeking whom he may devour" (1 Peter 5:8, emphasis added). If we ignore this warning, we become vulnerable to subtle, unpredictable assaults of Satan.

Take, for example, the issue of vacations. Ruth and I have found that we cannot continue our ministry effectively unless we pause from time to time to take a few days off and to wait upon God. (Our holidays really are *holy days*.) But I have learned one thing: *Satan never takes a holiday*. Just when we feel our greatest need to relax, Satan releases some totally unanticipated pressure against us and we may easily be caught without our weapons ready for immediate use.

Does that mean, then, that we no longer take vacations? No! But it means that we do not *bury our faces*, even during these times of relaxation; we do not lay down our weapons. We have learned, in fact, that these are often times when we need to exercise the greatest vigilance.

This is just one example that applies to many different areas: family relationships, business activities, special celebrations, educational opportunities. We can participate in all of these, but we must not *bury our faces* in any of them.

Remember, in Gideon's army, fewer than one out of four hundred qualified! Would the proportions be different today?

Once we pass the test of vigilance, that is just the beginning. We look now at how our personalities affect our preparedness and, thus, define the next step in building the character of a soldier.

3

Requirements for God's Army

Now may the God of peace Himself sanctify you completely;
and may your whole spirit, soul, and body be preserved
blameless at the coming of our Lord Jesus Christ.

1 Thessalonians 5:23

It is Paul's prayer that Christians be *completely* sanctified, and he then specifies the three areas that make up total human personality: spirit, soul and body.

The distinctions of each of these three elements of our personalities are little understood by most Christians. Yet the Bible provides us with a unique kind of "mirror" that reveals their nature and interrelationship, and shows us how each is intended to function. Failure to use this mirror correctly exposes us to much inner frustration and disharmony.

In the initial creation of man God said, "Let Us make man in Our *image*," and "according to Our *likeness*" (Genesis 1:26, emphasis added). *Image* refers to man's outward appearance. In a way that is not true of any other creature, man reflects the outward appearance of God. It was appropriate, therefore, that when the Son of God came to dwell on earth, it was in the form of a man—not an ox or a beetle—and not even in the form of some heavenly creature, such as a seraph.

Likeness refers to man's inner nature. Scripture refers to God as a triune being: Father, Son and Spirit. Likewise, it reveals that man is a triune being, consisting of spirit, soul and body. The account of man's creation reveals how his triune nature came into being: "And the LORD God formed man of the dust of the ground, and breathed into his nostrils the breath of life; and man became a living being"—more correctly, a living soul (Genesis 2:7).

Man's spirit came from the inbreathed breath of God. His body was formed from clay, transformed into living human flesh. Instantly he became a living soul.

The soul thus formed is the *ego*, the individual personality. It is usually defined as consisting of three elements: the will, the intellect and the emotions. It has the responsibility for making personal decisions and expresses itself in three phrases: "I want," "I think," "I feel." Unless touched by the supernatural grace of God, all of human behavior is controlled by these three motivations.

The Effects of Sin—and Salvation

Man was created for personal fellowship with God, but his sinful disobedience produced disastrous effects in all three elements of his personality.

Cut off from contact with God, man's *spirit* died. This was in fulfillment of God's warning: "But of the tree of the knowledge of good and evil you shall not eat, *for in the day that you eat of it you shall surely die*" (Genesis 2:17, emphasis added). Adam's *body*, now subject to corruption—that is, to sickness, decay and death—eventually ceased to function; he died more than nine hundred years later. Through exercising his will in direct disobedience to God, man became a rebel in his *soul*. Since that time, every person descended from Adam has inherited the nature of a rebel.

In Ephesians 2:1–3, Paul describes the results of rebellion that have affected every one of us:

> And you . . . were dead in trespasses and sins, in which you once walked according to the course of this world, according to the prince of the power of the air, the spirit who now works in the sons of disobedience [rebellion], among whom also we all once conducted ourselves in the lusts of our flesh, fulfilling the desires of the flesh and of the mind, and were by nature children of wrath, just as the others.

As a result of sin, we have all been dead in our spirits. In our souls we have all been in rebellion against God. Our bodies, too, have suffered the effects of sickness, decay and death.

Yet the boundless love of God is such that He continually longs for the restoration of His fellowship with man. "He jealously desires the Spirit which He has made to dwell in us" (James 4:5, NASB). Furthermore, through the sacrifice of Jesus on the cross, God has opened a way for the restoration of that fellowship which was lost.

Paul explains this outworking of salvation in our spirits: "But God, who is rich in mercy, because of His great love with which He loved us, even when we were dead in trespasses, made us alive together with Christ" (Ephesians 2:4–5). Our spirits, being reunited with God, are alive once more. At the same time, our souls—through repentance and faith—are released from rebellion and reconciled to God.

> For if when we were enemies we were reconciled to God through the death of His Son, much more, having been reconciled, we shall be saved by His life. And not only that, but we also rejoice in God through our Lord Jesus Christ, through whom we have now received the reconciliation.
>
> Romans 5:10–11

When we realize that we have all been in rebellion against God, we understand why there can be no genuine salvation without *repentance*. Repentance means laying down our rebellion and submitting ourselves to God's righteous government.

Salvation also makes provision for the body. Delivered from the slavery of sin, our bodies become temples in which the Holy Spirit dwells and our members become instruments of righteousness (see Romans 6:13). Finally, at the return of Christ, our bodies will be transformed into immortal bodies like that of Christ Himself!

Requirements for Discipleship

How does this apply to our engaging in spiritual battle? Jesus commissioned His apostles to make disciples of all nations. He did not tell them to make church members. After vigilance, which we embraced in our last study, the next step toward building the character of a soldier is discipleship, and it requires a radical response in each area of the personality—body, soul and spirit.

The requirement for our bodies is stated in Romans 12:1: "that you present your bodies a living sacrifice, holy, acceptable to God." We are required to offer our bodies upon the altar of sacrifice to God just as completely as the Israelites under the old covenant offered the animals they sacrificed on their altars. There is, however, one important difference. The Israelites *killed* the animals they offered to God. The body we offer to God is to be a *living* sacrifice.

Nevertheless, from that moment onward, our bodies no longer belong to us. They are God's property, God's temples. We are mere stewards who must give an account to God for the way in which we have cared for His temple. Unfortunately, far too many Christians today continue to treat their bodies as if they still own them and are free to do with them whatever they please.

Concerning our souls, Jesus stated His requirement in Matthew 16:24–25:

> "If anyone desires to come after Me, let him deny himself [literally, his soul], and take up his cross, and follow Me. For whoever desires to save his life [soul] will lose it, but whoever loses his life [soul] for My sake will find it."

Our cross is the place where we choose to die. God does not impose this upon us. We take it up only of our own free will. It is here that we must *deny our souls*. This means that we say no to the three demands of the soul: "I want," "I think," "I feel." Henceforth, we are no longer controlled by these three motives. Their place is taken by God's Word and God's will. As we obey the Word and the will of God, we find the new life that Jesus offers us. It is only through death that our souls can find this new life.

As we fulfill the Lord's requirements for our bodies and our souls, our spirits are liberated to enter into a fellowship with God that is even more wonderful than that which was lost through the Fall. Look at 1 Corinthians 6:15–16. Here Paul warns Christians against immoral sexual union with prostitutes, because this means becoming one body with the prostitute. Then, in direct contrast, he continues, *"But he who is joined to the Lord is one spirit with Him"* (verse 17, emphasis added).

The implication is clear. The redeemed spirit can now enjoy a union with God that is as close and intimate as sexual union is for the body. It is the spirit alone, however—not the soul or the body—that can experience this direct intimate union with God.

It is primarily through the act of worship that our spirits enter into this union. Jesus said: "The true worshipers will worship the Father *in spirit* and truth. . . . God is Spirit, and [all] those who worship Him must worship *in spirit* and truth" (John 4:23–24, emphasis added). He made it clear that true worship must be an activity of our spirits.

In the contemporary Church there is little understanding of the nature of worship, mainly because we do not discern the difference between the spirit and the soul. Worship is not entertainment. That belongs in the theater, not the church. Nor is worship the same as praise. We praise God with our souls, and it is right to do so. Through our praise we have access to God's presence. But once we are in His presence, it is through worship that we enjoy true spiritual union with Him.

To be able to worship God in this way is the goal of salvation—first on earth, and then in heaven. It is the highest and holiest activity of which a human being is capable. It is only possible, however, when the soul and the body come into submission to the spirit and in harmony with it. Such worship is often too profound for words. It becomes an intense and silent union with God.

Since this distinction between spirit and soul is vital for effective discipleship, let's explore more deeply how to discern between the two.

4

Finding Inner Harmony

I n the original pattern of creation, man experienced
a "descending" relationship with God. That is, God
moved upon man's spirit, his spirit moved upon his soul
and his soul directed his body. The spirit of man that came
directly from God, related directly to God. Through man's
rebellion, however, his spirit was set aside and his soul
took control. As a result, unregenerate man is controlled
by the three functions of his soul: the will, the intellect and
the emotions.

When God reconciles man to Himself, His purpose is to
restore the original order, by which He once again relates
directly to man's spirit; man's spirit in turn moves upon his
soul and man's soul moves upon his body. This explains
the words of David in Psalm 103:1: "Bless the LORD, O my
soul." Through faith, David's spirit had been reunited with
God and was eager to worship Him. So his spirit stirred

up his soul to move upon his vocal organs to utter the appropriate words of worship.

So long as man remains in submission to God and his soul remains in submission to his spirit, man functions in harmony with God and with himself. But if at any time man reasserts his rebellion against God, his soul is no longer in submission to his spirit and the inner harmony is broken. This means that there is constant tension between the spirit and the soul.

Which One Rules?

The Greek of the New Testament has a special adjective that describes action initiated by the soul. The word for *soul* is *psuche*, and the adjective formed from it is *psuchikos*. The natural way to render this in English would be *soulish*, but, unfortunately, English has not produced such a word. Consequently, English translations of the New Testament have used a variety of different words to express it: *natural* (KJV, NKJV), *sensual* (NKJV), *worldly* (NKJV), *unspiritual* and *worldly-minded* (NASB), *without the spirit* (NIV) and the phrase, *to follow their natural instinct* (NIV). Most English readers do not realize that these seven different words or phrases all translate one and the same Greek word. In this book I will use the word *soulish* to define the New Testament word *psuchikos* or *of the soul*.

In 1 Corinthians 15:44–46, Paul uses this word three times to point out the difference between our present bodies, which are *natural* (*soulish*), and our resurrection bodies, which will be *spiritual*:

It is sown a natural body, it is raised a spiritual body. There is a natural body, and there is a spiritual body. And so it is written, "The first man Adam became a living being." The last Adam became a life-giving spirit. However, the spiritual is not first, but the natural, and afterward the spiritual.

Again, a *soulish* body is one upon which the spirit moves only by working through the soul. A *spiritual* body is one upon which the spirit moves directly, without having to work through the soul. This latter is apparently the kind of body that the cherubs, which are described in the first chapter of Ezekiel, have: "Each one went straight forward; they went wherever the spirit wanted to go" (verse 12). Again, "wherever the spirit wanted to go, they went, because there the spirit went" (verse 20).

This seems to be the type of body that Paul is saying believers will have after resurrection. No longer will our spirits have to urge our souls to direct our bodies to make appropriate responses. Our bodies will respond directly to the decisions of our spirits. We will be like Ezekiel's cherubs: We will go directly, without turning, wherever our spirits will to go. What glorious liberty!

There are three passages in the New Testament that explain more clearly the opposition or tension between the spiritual and the soulish. First, Paul says:

> But the natural [soulish] man does not receive the things of the Spirit of God, for they are foolishness to him; nor can he know them, because they are spiritually discerned. But he who is spiritual judges all things, yet he himself is rightly judged by no one.
>
> 1 Corinthians 2:14–15

For the understanding of spiritual things, the soul is dependent upon the spirit. If it is out of harmony with the spirit, the realm of spiritual truth is closed to it. How important it is, therefore, particularly for engagement in spiritual battle, that we approach truth with the right attitude—our souls submitted to our spirits and our spirits in union with God!

Second, in his epistle, Jude speaks about people in the church who are "grumblers, complainers, walking according to their own lusts . . . sensual [soulish] persons, who cause divisions, not having the [Holy] Spirit" (Jude 16, 19).

When the soul of a Christian is not submitted through his spirit to God, he becomes a channel through which every kind of carnality and divisiveness can infiltrate the Church. This is the true, underlying cause of divisions in the Body of Christ.

And finally, in James 3:15 the apostle speaks about a form of wisdom that "does not descend from above, but is earthly, sensual [soulish], demonic." James depicts a downward slide in three successive stages: from the *earthly* to the *soulish* to the *demonic.*

When Christians become *earthly,* they lose the vision of eternity. They cannot see beyond the things of this life: success, pleasure, wealth, physical health. They are interested only in what their faith will do for them in this life! Concerning such people Paul says: "If in this life only we have hope in Christ, we are of all men the most pitiable" (1 Corinthians 15:19). Christians like that often consider themselves prosperous and successful. God considers them pitiable.

After the *earthly,* the next stage is *soulish.* To be soulish is to be egocentric, self-centered. For such people, the Christian faith is a way to get what they want out of life. They suppose that "godliness is a means of gain" (1 Timothy 6:5).

The *soulish* opens the way for the *demonic.* This is one main way in which demons infiltrate the Church. The question is often asked: Do Christians ever need deliverance from demons? The words of James provide the answer. This downward slide from the earthly to the soulish to the demonic exposes both individual believers and whole congregations to the activities of demons.

Restoring Harmony

In many places today the Church is an ungodly mixture. No clear line is drawn between the spiritual and the soulish, and there is, therefore, no barrier to the demonic. Genuine manifestations of the Holy Spirit are interspersed with manifestations that are clearly demonic. As a result, many sincere believers are confused and bewildered.

To protect ourselves, we must cultivate scriptural discernment. We must learn to distinguish between what is truly spiritual and what is soulish. There is only one instrument that is sharp enough to do this: the Word of God. We will look further at the indispensable Word of God later in this book, but for now we acknowledge that

> the word of God is living and powerful, and sharper than any two-edged sword, piercing even to the division of soul and spirit, and of joints and marrow, and is a discerner of the thoughts and intents of the heart.
>
> Hebrews 4:12

Further on, in Hebrews 5:14, the writer states two conditions that we must fulfill in order to exercise this kind of discernment: "But solid food belongs to those who are of full age, that is, those who by reason of use [practice] have their senses exercised to discern both good and evil."

The first condition is that we must regularly feed on *solid spiritual food* through the study of *the whole Bible*. The second condition is that we must regularly *practice* discernment. We must be continually alert, recognizing the spiritual forces that we encounter in every situation every day. Discernment should be as much a part of the Christian soldier's life as prayer.

I received this letter from a German psychiatrist who had a revelation of the "spiritual" and "soulish" areas of his personality. It gives an idea of the changes this discernment can make in one's life:

Dear Mr. Prince:

Never in my life has this happened to me before. While listening to your lecture [on "What Is Man?"], I saw for the first time in my Christian life the "spiritual Hans" of me somehow elevated as if on a chair and looking down onto the "soulish Hans" whose monument-like appearance seemed to crumble away.

Regenerated, this spiritual part of me, the "spiritual Hans," has survived ever since I listened to your lecture—fueled by the Holy Spirit—about five weeks ago. The "soulish Hans" of me—in particular, its intellectual and emotional areas—*must be dragged to the cross.*

You will understand that this change in my life—this being again a "triune" human being—is about to revolutionize even my profession. And for the first time in my life—now 45 years old—I see some good reason in having become a psychiatrist.

Hans P., Germany

We will not have true spiritual bodies until the resurrection. For now, however, we can, like Hans, prepare for service by remaining submissive to God and training our souls to stay in submission to our spirits. Finally, let us obey the exhortation of Paul in 1 Corinthians 16:13–14: "Watch, stand fast in the faith, be brave, be strong. Let all that you do be done with love."

Now let's look at how we maintain that level of service.

5

Testing vs. Chastening

It is vitally important that we learn to distinguish between God's testing and His chastening. As we will discover in this chapter, testing is a time for rejoicing and chastening is a time for repenting. We need to understand the difference between the two because our response depends on the particular way God is working. We will begin with testing.

Testing by God

"What is man . . . that You should visit him every morning, and test him every moment?" (Job 7:17–18).

Isn't that an amazing revelation—that God visits us every morning and tests us every moment? When it first became real to me, I had to ask myself: *Am I prepared to receive a visit from God every morning? Do I wake up with that expectation?*

Then I went on to ask myself: *Why does God test us? What is His purpose?*

Collins English Dictionary gives an interesting definition of the verb *test*: "To ascertain the worth of a person . . . by subjection to certain examinations." God does not test us because He is angry with us or wants to put us down. On the contrary, testing is a mark of God's favor. He tests us because He wants to establish our value. A jeweler will subject gold or silver to certain tests. He does this because they are valuable. He does not bother to test base metals such as iron or tin. Peter, in fact, compares our faith to gold, the genuineness of which must be tested by fire (see 1 Peter 1:7).

In the world of the patriarchs there was one man of outstanding righteousness who faced enormous testing. This book opened with a reference to his heart—the kind of heart that we seek in building our own character. His name was Job. God was proud of Job. He actually boasted about him to Satan: "Have you considered My servant Job, that there is none like him on the earth, a blameless and upright man, one who fears God and shuns evil?" (Job 1:8).

Characteristically, Satan's response was to attribute selfish motives to Job: "He only serves You because of what he gets from You."

In response, God permitted Satan to put Job to the test. First, He allowed Satan to destroy everything that belonged to Job: his possessions, his servants and his children. Then God even permitted Satan to touch Job's body—to afflict him with boils from head to toe. But He did not permit Satan to take Job's life.

Job recognized that God was testing him. "When He has tested me," he said, "I shall come forth as gold" (Job 23:10)—that is, gold that had been tested by fire. This gave him the strength to endure. He cried out in agony of soul, but he never gave up.

Typically, Eliphaz and Job's other two religious friends concluded that Job's sufferings were due to sins he had committed and they brought all sorts of terrible accusations against him. In the end, however, God vindicated Job and rebuked his friends. He told Eliphaz, "You have not spoken of Me what is right, as My servant Job has" (Job 42:7).

Abraham, another of our patriarchs who had a heart perfect toward God, was also a righteous man who was subjected to severe tests—even to the point of being required to offer his son to God as a burnt offering. Abraham was subjected to special tests because he had a special destiny—to become the father of God's chosen people, both Jewish and Christian. God applies special tests to those for whom He has special purposes.

The New Testament clearly warns us that, as Christians, we must expect to undergo testing. James tells us that we should respond to this testing with joy:

My brethren, count it all joy when you fall into various trials, knowing that the testing of your faith produces patience [endurance]. But let patience [endurance] have its perfect work, that you may be perfect and complete, lacking nothing.

James 1:2–4

On different occasions Ruth and I have each had to repent and ask God's forgiveness because we did not respond rightly to some of our tests. We did not count them all joy!

James gives us further understanding of this concept of testing, referring to the life of Job: "You have heard of the endurance of Job and have seen the outcome of the Lord's dealings, that the Lord is full of compassion and is merciful" (James 5:11, NASB). Testing, then, is an occasion of joy for the Christian, a time of building character in which the Lord's compassion and mercy will be evident.

Now what about chastening?

Chastening by God

Many people seem to assume that once they become Christians they are exempt from God's chastening—especially if they have been believers for any length of time. This attitude, however, has no basis in Scripture. To such believers Hebrews gives a powerful warning:

> And you have forgotten the exhortation which speaks to you as to sons: "My son, do not despise the chastening of the LORD, nor be discouraged when you are rebuked by Him; for whom the LORD loves He chastens, and scourges every son whom He receives." If you endure chastening, God deals with you as with sons; for what son is there whom a father does not chasten? But if you are without chastening, of which all have become partakers, then you are illegitimate and not sons.
>
> Hebrews 12:5–8

In this connection, God impressed upon me the example of His dealings with Moses. Moses was eighty years old when the Lord commissioned him to return to Egypt and deliver Israel from their slavery. Yet when Moses was on his way back to Egypt, the Lord met him and actually sought to kill him (see Exodus 4:24–26)!

Why such chastening? Because of Moses' disobedience. Moses had not fulfilled the covenant of circumcision, which the Lord had made with Abraham and his descendants (see Genesis 17:9–14). Only when Moses repented and had his son circumcised did the Lord spare Moses' life and release him to go on his way. God would rather have killed Moses than permit him to go through with his mission in disobedience. His position as a leader did not exempt him from God's discipline. It made him all the more accountable.

For me, in my 82nd year at this writing, there is a personal application. I cannot expect to complete my God-given assignment if I make room for disobedience in my life. When we come under the dealings of God, we need to humble ourselves before Him and pray the prayer of David in Psalm 139:23–24: "Search me, O God, and know my heart; test me and know my anxious thoughts. See if there is any offensive way in me, and lead me in the way everlasting" (NIV).

What God reveals will determine how we respond. Our response to chastening should be to *repent*; our response to testing should be to *endure*. If we persist in trying to endure when we should repent, we are guilty of insensitivity and stubbornness. We are adopting a posture of resisting the devil when we should in fact be submitting to God. The root character problem that this exposes is *pride*.

There is a prayer at the end of Psalm 19 that Ruth and I often repeat:

> Who can understand his errors?
> Cleanse me from secret faults.
> Keep back Your servant also from presumptuous sins;
> Let them not have dominion over me.
> Then I shall be blameless,
> And I shall be innocent of great transgression.
>
> Psalm 19:12–13

I have come to see that *secret faults* are not secrets that we keep from other people—much less from God. They are secret to ourselves, faults in our own character that we do not recognize. David describes them as "presumptuous sins"—sins that we commit when we *presume* that our conduct is acceptable to God, when in fact it offends Him.

Very often God will not reveal such sins to us until we deliberately choose to humble ourselves and invite Him to search our character and to lay bare our inmost motives. If we sincerely allow the Lord to search our hearts and

He does not put His finger on anything that is offensive to Him, then we may conclude that we are under God's testing, not His chastening.

Not Sure Which?

As Christians we will all undergo tests and chastening. They may come in many different forms: a crisis in our health or finances; a breakdown in a personal relationship; rejection or persecution because of our faith; some long, dark tunnel with no light at the other end. Sometimes we will know how the hand of God is working and sometimes we may not be 100 percent certain. In that case, I find that it helps to make sure that "all our bases are covered" (to borrow a phrase from baseball). Here, briefly, are steps to take.

Base Number 1: Repentance

Repentance is perhaps the basic Christian doctrine least emphasized by contemporary preachers. "Only believe" is a sweet-sounding message, but it is not scriptural. From the beginning to the end of the New Testament, the message is this: *First repent, then believe.* We must ask God to reveal any sin that may be present in our lives. If we are open to His leading, He will make it clear. Otherwise, any kind of faith that does not proceed out of repentance is a humanistic counterfeit. It does not produce the results that proceed from genuine faith.

A simple illustration of true repentance is making a U-turn in a vehicle. You recognize that you have not been living the right way. You stop and make a U-turn. After that you proceed in the opposite direction. If you do not end up traveling in the opposite direction, you have not truly repented.

Base Number 2: Commitment

According to Romans 10:9 there are two essential conditions for salvation: to believe in our hearts that God raised Jesus from the dead; to confess with our mouths Jesus as Lord.

When we confess Jesus as Lord, we give Him unreserved control over our whole lives—our time, our money, our talents, our priorities, our relationships. We cannot hold anything back. "If Jesus is not Lord of all"—someone has said—"then He is not Lord at all."

Base Number 3: Attitude toward Scripture

Satan brought about the downfall of our first parents when he enticed them into questioning the truth of God's Word: "Has God indeed said . . . ?" (Genesis 3:1).

Jesus Himself set the seal of His divine authority upon Scripture when He called it "the word of God" and added that "the Scripture cannot be broken" (John 10:35). Paul stated categorically, "All Scripture is given by inspiration of God" (2 Timothy 3:16).

To question the authority of Scripture is a luxury that none of us can afford. It is the path to disaster today just as surely as it was in the Garden of Eden.

Base Number 4: Right Relationships

Right doctrine is the basis of the Christian faith. But right doctrine rightly applied will produce right relationships. Our personal relationships should reflect the doctrine that we profess.

Jesus laid great emphasis on maintaining right relationships. He gave clear guidelines for dealing with a brother who sins against us (see Matthew 18:15–17). In the Sermon on the Mount, He warned, "Agree with your adversary quickly, while you are on the way with him" (Matthew 5:25). And He closed His model prayer with a solemn warning: "But if you do not forgive men their trespasses, neither will your Father forgive your trespasses" (Matthew 6:15).

In any time of testing or chastening we should be careful to check our attitudes and our relationships, to make sure that we are not harboring any bitterness or resentment or unforgiveness in our hearts.

We also need to bear in mind that we cannot have right relationships with the wrong people. "Do not be deceived," Paul states. "Evil company corrupts good habits" (1 Corinthians 15:33). We cannot lead holy lives if we deliberately consort with unholy people. All such relationships must be cut off with the sharp sword of God's Word.

What Is God Looking For?

Through His instruments of testing and chastening, God is building important character traits in us: trust and endurance. The subject of endurance, a topic vital to surviving spiritual battle, flows throughout this book. It will be covered in depth in Part 4, but we will look at it briefly here.

Trust

The basic issues of sin or righteousness are defined in Satan's original temptation of Adam and Eve. His Greek title *diabolos* (English *devil*) means "slanderer." To slander someone means to "defame his character." This is Satan's primary activity.

First and foremost, Satan defames the character of God Himself. Hence, in his original question to Eve, "Has God indeed said, 'You shall not eat of every tree of the garden'?"

(Genesis 3:1), Satan implied that God was a despot—arbitrary, unfair and unloving. God was shutting Adam and Eve out from a "higher level" of knowledge that would open up to them if they tasted of the fruit of the tree of the knowledge of good and evil. Satan's goal was to undermine their trust in God's goodness when, in fact, God had already provided them with everything that was good, beautiful and delightful.

From mistrust of God's goodness, Adam and Eve moved to disbelief in God's word and then to the act of disobedience. These were the three stages in their fall: *mistrust, disbelief* and *disobedience.*

Through faith in Christ, God has provided redemption that reverses the downward process of the Fall. It replaces disbelief with faith, disobedience with obedience, and mistrust with trust. Faith leading to obedience is the first stage. But the process is not complete until faith has developed into trust.

What is the difference between faith and trust? A non-theological answer would be: faith is an *act*; trust is an *attitude.* (It was British evangelist Smith Wigglesworth who continually emphasized that faith is an act.) A clear illustration of the difference between faith as an act and trust as an attitude is provided in Psalm 37:5: "Commit your way to the LORD, trust also in Him, and He will do it" (NASB). *Commit* describes a single act of faith; *trust* describes a continuing attitude that follows the initial act of committing. After that, God takes over: *He will do it.*

A simple illustration would be making a deposit in a savings bank. You hand your money to the teller and receive a receipt. That is *committing*—an act of *faith.* After that, you do not lie awake at night wondering: *Is the bank really taking care of my money? Am I receiving the interest due to me?* You just put the receipt in a safe place and sleep soundly. That is *trust.* Many Christians take the first step, an act of faith, but do not maintain an attitude of trust. Strangely, many of us find it easier to trust an earthly bank than to trust God in heaven!

God uses testing and chastening, therefore, to produce trust in us. This was true of Job. In the midst of all his trials he affirmed: "Though He slay me, yet will I trust Him" (Job 13:15). That attitude of trust momentarily enabled Job to lift his eyes above the realm of time and to catch a glimpse of eternity and the resurrection:

> "For I know that my Redeemer lives, and He shall stand at last on the earth; and after my skin is destroyed, this I know, that in my flesh I shall see God, whom I shall see for myself, and my eyes shall behold, and not another. How my heart yearns within me!"
>
> Job 19:25–27

Why is trust so important? Because it reveals our *estimate of God's character*. When Adam and Eve yielded to Satan's temptation, their actions spoke louder than any words they might have uttered. They were saying: "God is not just and loving. He is not dealing fairly with us. He is not to be trusted."

Our salvation from sin is not complete until it has undone the effects of the Fall and produced in us this quality of *trust*. This may require us to go through many tests. It is important that we never lose sight of God's end purpose: to produce in us an unshakable confidence in His absolute trustworthiness.

Jesus has provided us with the supreme example of trust. In fulfillment of His Father's plan, He was handed over to wicked, cruel and godless men. They mocked Him, spat on Him, flogged Him, stripped Him naked and nailed Him to a cross. Eventually He cried out, "My God, My God, why have You forsaken Me?" (Matthew 27:46). Yet in all this His trust in His Father's faithfulness never failed. With His last breath He yielded His spirit back to the Father.

47

How do we respond if we cry out to God and He does not seem to answer us? Can we still trust His faithfulness?

God will not permit us to be tested beyond what we can bear. He will not expect of us what He required of Jesus—perhaps not even what He required of Job. Every test or corrective chastening we go through is designed to mold our character, until we have become in Christ all that God created us to be. "Blessed is the man who endures temptation [testing]; for when he has been approved, he will receive the crown of life" (James 1:12).

Endurance

One essential character requirement throughout Scripture is *endurance*. With many Christians, however, this is not a popular subject. If in my preaching I announce that my theme is to be endurance, I hear very few "Hallelujahs" in response. Sometimes I go on to say, "Let me tell you how to cultivate endurance." People listen eagerly, anxious to learn the secret. "There is only one way to cultivate endurance," I continue, "it is by enduring." This is greeted by an almost audible collective sigh. Expressed in words, that sigh says, "You mean there isn't any other easier way?"

No, there is no easier way! Endurance is an essential element of victorious Christian living, and it can only be cultivated by enduring. Once we accept this fact, we can begin to respond rightly to each difficulty that comes our way. We can "count it all joy . . . knowing that the testing of [our] faith produces patience [endurance]" (James 1:2–3).

But we are warned that we must "let patience [endurance] have its perfect work" (James 1:4). In other words, we must continue to endure until God's purpose has been fully worked out and He brings the trial to an end.

48

Very seldom does God tell us in advance, "This challenge will last six months." So it may happen that after five and a half months a person will say, "I can't take any more of this; I give up!"

How sad! Another fifteen days of enduring and God's purpose would have been accomplished. Yet now such a person will have to undergo another challenge, designed to deal with the same character defect. In fact, God will not withdraw His tests and chastening until His purpose has been accomplished. The sooner we learn to endure—assuming repentance has taken place when necessary—the more rapid will be our spiritual progress.

Paul—like the writer of Hebrews—uses the example of an athlete to describe endurance: "And everyone who competes for the prize is temperate [exercises self-control] in all things" (1 Corinthians 9:25). Only if we cultivate self-control will we have the strength to endure.

In 2 Peter 1:5–7, we find seven successive "steps" that lead upward from the foundation of *faith* to the supreme completion of Christian character: *agape love*. These steps are:

virtue (moral excellence)
knowledge
self-control
perseverance (endurance)
godliness
brotherly kindness
love

Peter makes it clear that self-control is an essential prerequisite for endurance. Every test of endurance is also a test of self-control. It will expose any weakness in any one of the various areas of our personality. In the area of the emotions, the weakness may be fear or discouragement or depression. In our fleshly nature, it may be unbridled lusts or appetites. In our personal relationships, it may be anger or jealousy. In our spiritual development, it may be pride or self-confidence.

Whatever the area of weakness may be, it will be exposed when we are confronted with the challenge to endure. It is a tragic fact that many Christians never overcome these two stages of self-control and endurance. Consequently, they never progress to the higher Christian virtues in the remaining three steps: *godliness, brotherly kindness, love.*

Looking to Jesus

The supreme example of right responses to testing is provided by Jesus Himself, of course, who "was in all points tempted [tested] as we are, yet without sin" (Hebrews 4:15). To follow His example requires that we "lay aside every weight, and the sin which so easily ensnares us, and . . . run with endurance the race that is set before us, looking unto Jesus, the author and finisher [perfecter] of our faith" (Hebrews 12:1–2).

It is not sufficient that we deal with things in our lives that are actually sinful. We must also eliminate *weights*—things that are not sinful in themselves, but yet would hinder us from concentrating every effort on our service for Christ.

A runner in a race strips down to the bare minimum. He does not carry one ounce of unnecessary weight. We must do the same. Here are some of the things that we may need to eliminate: social obligations that have no spiritual significance; sentimental attachments to people, places or pets; excessive concern with the stock market, sports or women's fashions; window shopping; worries about money, health, family or politics.

Concerning each thing to which we devote time and attention, we need to ask two questions: Does it glorify Jesus? Does it build me up spiritually?

Or does it build me up personally? This pitfall is the topic of our next chapter.

6

The Hardest Test of All

If I were to ask a group of people, *What would you consider the hardest test that Christians face?* I would probably receive a variety of different answers. My own answer may surprise you, but it is based on more than fifty years in full-time Christian ministry. I believe that the hardest test we are likely to face—and the one we are least likely to pass—is *success.*

Solomon warns us: "The end of a thing is better than its beginning; the patient in spirit is better than the proud in spirit" (Ecclesiastes 7:8). To put it another way: It is not how you start a race that makes you a winner, but how you finish it. A veteran Chinese pastor, who spent more than twenty years in prison for his faith and recently went to be with the Lord, made this personal comment: "I have seen many people have good beginnings, but few have good endings." I can say the same.

As examples of men who have achieved success, we will consider some of the kings of Israel.

Old Testament Kings

The first king, Saul, was a strong, outstanding young man, who early in his career gained various military victories. But when sent by God on a mission against the Amalekites, he allowed fear of the people to keep him from full obedience to God's command. As a result, the prophet Samuel came to him with a message that God had rejected him as king.

Saul's root problem was summed up in Samuel's message: "When you were *little in your own eyes*, were you not head of the tribes of Israel?" (1 Samuel 15:17, emphasis added). As long as Saul remained humble, God could bless him. But when he became proud, God had to set him aside.

This applies to all of us. When we are little in our own eyes, we have room for the greatness of God. But when we become great in our own eyes, we leave no room for God to manifest His greatness through us.

Saul's pride drove him to a tragic end. The last night of his life he consulted a witch, and the following day he committed suicide on the battlefield.

The next king, David, was a man after God's heart. For years he had to live as a fugitive, persecuted and hounded by King Saul. Yet, he came through it all victoriously and eventually he had a wonderful testimony:

The LORD rewarded me according to my righteousness; according to the cleanness of my hands He has recompensed me. For I have kept the ways of the LORD, and have not wickedly departed from my God.

Psalm 18:20–21

But later David changed, and so did his language:

Have mercy upon me, O God, according to Your lovingkindness; according to the multitude of Your tender mercies, blot out my transgressions. Wash me thoroughly from my iniquity, and cleanse me from my sin.

Psalm 51:1–2

What had happened? Why the change? David had experienced total *success*. Established as king over all Israel, victorious over all his enemies, he was enjoying the fruits of success. He no longer went out to battle. He remained at home in Jerusalem, free to indulge in all that took his fancy.

So he did not hesitate to seduce Bathsheba, the wife of his neighbor Uriah. Nor to procure the murder of Uriah to cover up his sin. In David's time of success, he forgot the principles he lived by before he became king.

Thank God that David eventually repented and God forgave his sin! Nevertheless, David's sin cast a dark shadow over his descendants from generation to generation. God warned him: "Now therefore, the sword shall never depart from your house" (2 Samuel 12:10). It is important for all of us to remember that God's *forgiveness* does not necessarily cancel all the *consequences* of our sins.

David's son Solomon, who succeeded him as king, was beloved and chosen by God. Because he humbly acknowledged his need of wisdom, God also gave him riches and honor. He became the wisest, richest and most famous of all Israel's kings.

Yet in spite of all his wisdom, Solomon did not pass the test of success.

For it was so, when Solomon was old, that his wives turned his heart after other gods. . . . For Solomon went after Ashtoreth the goddess of the Sidonians, and after Milcom

the abomination of the Ammonites. Solomon did evil in
the sight of the LORD.

1 Kings 11:4–6

In spite of his glorious beginning, Solomon died an
idolater.

Following Solomon, the kingdom was divided. *All* the
kings of Israel, the northern kingdom, became idolaters and
were rejected by the Lord. Many of the kings of the south-
ern kingdom, Judah, also turned away from the Lord into
idolatry. There were, however, some truly righteous kings
in Judah. Yet none of them fully passed the test of *success.*

Hezekiah, for example, introduced sweeping reforms
and reestablished the true worship of Jehovah. When
Sennacherib, king of Assyria, laid siege to Jerusalem, the
Lord intervened and granted a miraculous deliverance to
Hezekiah and his people. Later, when Hezekiah was sick
to the point of death, God not only healed him, but granted
him a miraculous sign by reversing the course of the sun.
He also promised Hezekiah fifteen extra years of life.

The miraculous sign in the sun extended Hezekiah's
fame to other nations. As a result, ambassadors came from
Babylon. Flattered by their attention, Hezekiah showed
them everything of value in his whole kingdom. But he
did not give God the glory!

Scripture provides two illuminating comments on
Hezekiah's conduct:

> But Hezekiah did not repay according to the favor shown
> him, for his heart was lifted up [he became proud]. . . .
> However, regarding the ambassadors of the princes of
> Babylon, whom they sent to him to inquire about the won-
> der that was done in the land, God withdrew from him,
> in order to test him, that He might know all that was in
> his heart.
>
> 2 Chronicles 32:25, 31

From Hezekiah we can learn two things. First, if God grants you some special miracle, that does not make you a special person; it only means that you have a special God. Second, if God withdraws His presence and does not seem to be actively at work in your life, it can mean that He is testing you to see how you will behave when left to yourself.

Later in Judah's history there arose another righteous king—Josiah. Like Hezekiah, Josiah also introduced radical reforms and restored the true worship of Jehovah. He also destroyed the idolatrous altar at Bethel in the northern kingdom.

But Josiah's successes made him self-confident, and he became rash. Without consulting the Lord and in the face of solemn warning, he opposed Pharaoh Necho, king of Egypt, and was killed in battle (see 2 Kings 23:29). With him the last flicker of hope for Judah died also.

Successful Men in the New Testament

What about the New Testament? Does it provide different standards? Let us look at the foremost personalities: Jesus Himself and three of His leading disciples, Peter, John and Paul. What about their endings?

Jesus, of course, is unique—the perfect, sinless Son of God. He never experienced failure. Yet He ended His life hanging naked on a cross, exposed to mocking sinners. That was the last the "world" saw of Jesus. His subsequent resurrection, and the glory that followed, were revealed only to "witnesses chosen before by God" (Acts 10:41). As far as the world is concerned, Jesus was perhaps a good teacher, even a good man, but hardly a great success, and God has never sought to set the record straight.

What about Peter, the leader of the twelve apostles? According to reliable tradition, Peter, too, ended his life on a cross—crucified head downward, at his own request, because he did not feel worthy to suffer in the same way as his Lord.

We have no reliable record of the death of John. But we do know that in his old age he was banished to the barren, rocky island of Patmos, where he received the visions recorded in the book of Revelation.

What about Paul? We have his own record of how he and his fellow apostles lived:

> To this very hour we go hungry and thirsty, we are in rags, we are brutally treated, we are homeless. We work hard with our own hands. When we are cursed, we bless; when we are persecuted, we endure it; when we are slandered, we answer kindly. Up to this moment we have become the scum of the earth, the refuse of the world.
>
> 1 Corinthians 4:11–13, NIV

Finally, after a powerful and miraculous ministry that opened up the Gentile world to the Gospel, Paul ended in chains in a cold Roman dungeon, forsaken by some of his closest co-workers. From there he was taken out for public execution by beheading.

Do these records of Jesus, Peter, John and Paul mean that all committed Christians must necessarily die the death of martyrs? Or that no committed Christian could ever be wealthy? No! But they do enforce one extremely important point: *We must never let the world entice us into accepting its standards of success.* We must never seek the world's approval. The desire for popularity is always dangerous.

Jesus gave some strong warnings against this. To the Pharisees He said: "For what is highly esteemed among men is an abomination in the sight of God" (Luke 16:15). To His own disciples He said: "Woe to you when all men speak well of you, for so did their fathers to the false prophets" (Luke 6:26).

The Key to True Success

Mentally I contrasted the endings of those five kings in the Old Testament with those of Jesus and His disciples. *What is the key*—I asked—*to building a character of true success?* The Lord directed me to two Scriptures.

First, the words of Paul in 1 Corinthians 7:25: "I give my judgment, as one that hath obtained mercy of the Lord to be faithful" (KJV). I saw that to be faithful *I must be totally dependent on the Lord's mercy.* I cannot rely on anything else: my academic background, my spiritual gifts, my past achievements, my years in Christian service. There is only one thing that can keep me faithful: *the mercy of God.* I must make it the central purpose of my life to be consciously and continually dependent on God's mercy. I must be on my guard against anything that would blur or dull my sense of dependence. Particularly, I must be watchful for any form of pride, which is, in essence, self-dependence.

Second, the words of Jesus in John 4:34: "My food is to do the will of Him who sent Me, and to finish His work." Jesus' food—the source of His life and strength—was His single-minded determination to do God's will right through to the end of His life. That is the *true success* you and I must aim for.

7

Denying the "Old Man"

Success, we have just seen, has different meanings for different people. To the world it usually means riches and fame. To the Christian, it means doing the will of God. How do we achieve such success? There is only one way: *by following Jesus.* That is the way that a Christian builds character. It is, in fact, the essence of the Christian life.

This is illustrated by the conversion of Matthew the tax collector (see Matthew 9:9). As Matthew sat in his tax office, Jesus passed by and spoke two words: "Follow Me." Matthew's eternal destiny depended on his response. He arose and followed Jesus.

If we decide to respond as Matthew did, we discover that there are two essential preconditions before we can begin to follow. In his gospel, Matthew quotes Jesus as saying, "If anyone desires to come after Me, let him deny himself, and take up his cross, and follow Me" (Matthew 16:24). First, we must deny ourselves; second, we must take up our crosses.

To deny is to say no! We must say no to our insistent, demanding, self-assertive ego. We must echo the prayer of Jesus in Gethsemane: "Not My will, but Yours, be done" (Luke 22:42). Only after we have denied ourselves can we go on to take up our crosses. Someone has defined our crosses as the place where God's will and our will cross. It is, in fact, the place of execution.

In Romans 6:6, Paul tells us that "our old man was crucified with Him [Jesus]." Remember, we learned in our very first chapter that the old man is the rebellious, self-pleasing nature that each of us has inherited by descent from our common ancestor, Adam. God has only one solution for dealing with our old man. He does not send him to church or Sunday school; He does not teach him the Golden Rule or direct him to a class on self-improvement. God's solution is simple and final. It is execution.

The good news of the Gospel, however, is that the execution took place when Jesus died on the cross. Our old man was crucified at that time in Him. This is a simple historical fact. It is true whether or not we know it or believe it. But to benefit from it, we must both know it and believe it.

Challenged by God in a Dream

Nearly fifty years ago I used to conduct evangelistic meetings in London at Speaker's Corner, Marble Arch. One night during that period I had a vivid dream in which I saw a man preaching at Speaker's Corner. The man's message was good, but there was something about his appearance I did not like. His body was crooked and he seemed to have a clubfoot. At the time I did not attach any particular importance to my dream.

About a week later I had precisely the same dream. I concluded that God was saying something to me. "Lord," I asked, "who is that man? His preaching was good, but there was something I didn't like about his appearance. Who is he?"

The Lord's answer was immediate and direct: *You are the man!* God was evidently requiring some important changes from me, but I did not know what.

The Easter season was at hand and I found myself meditating on the crucifixion. I had a mental picture of three crosses on a hill. The central cross was higher than the other two.

For whom was that central cross made? the Holy Spirit asked me. But then He cautioned, *Be careful how you answer.*

I thought it over for a while, then I said, "The central cross was made for Barabbas—but at the last moment Jesus took his place."

So Jesus took the place of Barabbas, the Holy Spirit continued. *But you have said that Jesus took* your *place.*

"Yes, He did," I responded.

Then you must be Barabbas!

At that moment I saw it with absolute clarity: I was the criminal for whom the cross was prepared. It was made to my measure. That was where I should have been.

Even though my "old man" was crucified at the cross of Christ, I was still compelled to identify with Paul's assessment of himself: "For I know that in me (that is, in my flesh) nothing good dwells" (Romans 7:18). Every area of my personality was permeated, I saw, by the corruption of sin. There was nothing in me that was pure, that was good, that could merit God's favor.

So how was I to respond?

God's Provisions, Our Steps

In Romans 6:6–13, Paul sets out four successive steps we must take in order to build the character that defeats the old man and emulates Jesus' character.

1. First of all, I must *know* that my sinful nature was put to death when Jesus died on the cross. This is the essential first step from which all the rest follow. (See verse 6.)
2. I must *reckon*—consider—myself dead, just as Jesus was dead. (See verse 11.)
3. On that basis, I must refuse resolutely to let sin continue to dominate me. (See verse 12.)
4. I must present myself to God like someone raised from the dead, and I must yield my physical members as instruments (literally, weapons) of righteousness. The use of the word *weapons* alerted me that I would face opposition from Satan. (See verse 13.)

Thus, we see that to provide complete deliverance from the tyranny of sin required a threefold provision of God. First of all, He had to deal with our *sins*—the sinful acts we have all committed. Because Jesus on the cross has paid the full penalty for our sins, God can forgive us without compromising His own justice. His first provision, therefore, is *forgiveness*.

Then God had also to deal with the corrupt nature within us that caused us to go on committing those sinful acts. His provision was *execution*—to put that sinful nature to death. The good news is that the execution took place more than nineteen centuries ago when Jesus died on the cross.

That, however, is not the end. God's purpose is to replace the sinful old man with a new man of His own creating. This provision is explained in Ephesians 4:22–24:

> Put off, concerning your former conduct, the old man . . . and be renewed in the spirit of your mind, and . . . put on the new man which was created according to God, in true righteousness and holiness.

Even as we follow Paul's steps above, we should not assume that the old man will accept passively his sentence of execution. On the contrary, he will at times struggle fiercely to regain his control over us. This explains Paul's words of warning in Colossians 3. In verse 3 he says, "For you died." But then in verse 5 he says, "Therefore put to death your members which are on the earth." We must stand in faith that the death of our old man is an accomplished fact and we must actively resist his attempts to regain control over us.

Unfortunately, many sincere Christians have never understood or availed themselves of this complete provision of God. They claim—and continue to claim—the forgiveness of their sins, but they do not know that God has also made provision for the old man to be put to death and for a new man to take his place. Consequently, their Christian life is a wearisome repetitive cycle: sinning—repenting—being forgiven—and then sinning again. . . . They never experience release from the domination of the old sinful nature.

This analysis of God's total provision for sin should lead us to make a personal spiritual inventory, in which we ask ourselves the following questions: Am I completely sure that all my sins have been forgiven? Have I been freed from the domination of my old carnal nature? Have I put on the new man who is created in righteousness and true holiness? Am I following Jesus?

A Glimpse of the Future

At the close of this age God is going to provide for Himself 144,000 Israelite followers of Messiah. He will send them forth into a world that is reeling under the impact of "the great tribulation" and they will reap a harvest of souls so vast "that no one could number" it.

Revelation 14:1–5 depicts these 144,000 after they have triumphantly completed their task and—in all probability—

sealed their testimony with their lifeblood. With the names of the Father and of the Son written on their foreheads, they are worshiping God with a song that sounds "like the roar of rushing waters and like a loud peal of thunder" (Revelation 14:2, NIV)—a song that no one else could learn.

What kind of people are they?

Their character is clearly delineated: They are sexually pure; in their mouth is no guile; they are without fault. How have they attained to such a faultless character? There is one simple answer: "They follow the Lamb wherever He goes" (verse 4).

Does that inspire you—as it inspires me—with a longing to follow Jesus more closely?

8

The Role of Worship

At the end of the last chapter, we got a glimpse of those who attain spotless character and worship triumphantly at the throne of God. God has been dealing with me about this topic of worship—and I believe He has given me new understanding. I have always realized that worship is one of the main themes of the Bible and something that is of tremendous importance for the Christian entering spiritual battle, but I never felt I had a real clear grasp of the nature of worship.

As I mentioned earlier, I believe that true worship is very different from what many contemporary churchgoers have become accustomed to. In many churches people talk about the "morning worship service." Without being critical, it has been my experience that in many of those churches not much true worship is taking place. So, for our final study in character building, I want to examine the steps to true worship as well as the nature of worship. And then I want to suggest to you the fruit of true worship, which may seem contradictory in a book on preparing for battle: It is rest.

Let's take a look at Psalm 95, and then I will offer you some comments on this important military strategy.

Come, let us sing for joy to the LORD;
let us shout aloud to the Rock of our salvation.
Let us come before him with thanksgiving
and extol him with music and song.
For the LORD is the great God,
the great King above all gods.
In his hand are the depths of the earth,
and the mountain peaks belong to him.
The sea is his, for he made it,
and his hands formed the dry land.
Come, let us bow down in worship,
let us kneel before the LORD our Maker;
for he is our God
and we are the people of his pasture,
the flock under his care.
Today, if you hear his voice,
do not harden your hearts as you did at Meribah,
as you did that day at Massah in the desert,
where your fathers tested and tried me,
though they had seen what I did.
For forty years I was angry with that generation;
I said, "They are a people whose hearts go astray,
and they have not known my ways."
So I declared on oath in my anger,
"They shall never enter my rest."

NIV

It is unusual to have a psalm that ends with such a negative statement as that, but as we will see in a moment, I believe there is a special reason.

Entering the Gates and Courts

Three actions are closely associated in this psalm: thanksgiving, praise and worship; yet they are distinct. I liken them somewhat to the way individual colors of the rainbow blend into one another. The first two actions are easily understood. Very simply, I would say that we *thank* God for what He does, particularly for what He does for us. We *praise* God for His greatness.

According to Psalm 95, we should offer our thanksgiving and praise with exuberance—sing, shout, extol Him with music and song. Scripture says, "Great is the LORD, and greatly to be praised" (Psalm 48:1). I believe it is hard for God to accept halfhearted praise. In fact, if we are not prepared to praise Him greatly, maybe we should not do it at all. That is the way of access, and I do not believe there is any access without it. The prophet Isaiah says: "Thou shalt call thy walls Salvation, and thy gates Praise" (Isaiah 60:18, KJV). In other words, if you want to come into salvation you have got to come in by the gate, and every gate is praise.

Psalm 95 also gives us reasons why we should praise God:

> For the LORD is the great God, the great King above all gods. In his hand are the depths of the earth, and the mountain peaks belong to him. The sea is his, for he made it, and his hands formed the dry land.
>
> verses 3–5, NIV

As we look at the whole created universe, we witness the wisdom and the greatness of the Creator. That should elicit a response of thanksgiving and praise from us.

These two actions, then, show how we approach God. We come into the gates with thanksgiving, and then we move farther into the courts with praise. But neither of them is worship.

Worship: Relating to God

Every word in the Bible, Old Testament and New, that means "worship" or is translated "worship" is always descriptive of an attitude. I think this is what God has been speaking to me about—that worship is primarily an attitude. Essentially, it is the way we relate to God regarding His holiness.

Of all the attributes of God—and they are many—the hardest for the human mind to understand is holiness because it has no parallel on earth. We can talk about the wisdom of God, and we know wise people. We can talk about the greatness of God, and we know great people. We can talk about the power of God, and we see demonstrations of power. But apart from God there is no demonstration of holiness; it is something that is unique to God and those who have received it from God.

In verses 6–7, the mood of Psalm 95 changes, and we get to what I believe is the heart of the matter: "Come, let us bow down in worship, let us kneel before the LORD our Maker" (NIV). As I see it, this purposeful worship is not the type of loud boisterousness that has become the norm; it is quietness.

We see that there are certain physical postures associated with worship. These are present all through Scripture and they indicate humility—bowing the head, bowing down the upper part of the body, extending the arms with hands reaching upward, and falling on one's face before the Lord. This last one is particularly relevant, because it is easy to question whether any person who has never been on his face before God has ever been very close to God. You would be hard-pressed to find any of the really notable individuals of the Bible who had not been on their faces before God. For myself, I practice it—not as a matter of legalism or ritual, but from time to time when I feel I need security. The most secure place I know is on my face before God. John Bunyan said, "He that is down need fear no fall." When you are on the floor, there is no lower you can go. Jesus said that everyone who humbles himself shall be exalted; likewise, everyone who exalts himself shall be humbled (see Matthew 23:12).

In verse 7 of Psalm 95, we are given two reasons why we should worship the Lord: "For he is our God and we are the people of his pasture, the flock under his care" (NIV).

The first reason to worship God is because He *is* God and He is *our* God. He is the only being in the universe actually worthy of worship. We can praise men and women, but we must never worship men and women. Worship is the most distinctive way we have to relate to God as God.

I have become convinced that whatever we worship gains control of us. The more we worship it, the more like it we become—and the more it gains power over us. If we don't worship God, how much is He really our God?

The second reason given for worshiping Him is that we are the people of His pasture, the flock under His care. Worship is the appropriate response to God's care for us. It is the way we recognize Him as our God; it is the way we respond to His care for us.

Making the Choice

It is significant that the psalm does not end there. As we noted above, it ends with a solemn warning:

> Today, if you hear his voice,
>   do not harden your hearts as you did at Meribah. . . .
>   [Then God discusses that generation.]
> For forty years I was angry with that generation;
>   I said, "They are a people whose hearts go astray,
>   and they have not known my ways."
> So I declared on oath in my anger,
>   "They shall never enter my rest."
>
> Psalm 95:7–8, 10–11, NIV

This sets before us two alternatives: choosing to enter into true worship or choosing not to. In Jeremiah 7:23, God says to His people: "But this is what I commanded them, saying, 'Obey My voice, and I will be your God'" (NASB).

That is one of the simplest statements I have ever read of what God requires. "Obey My voice, and I will be your God."

In Deuteronomy 28 we find all the blessings of obedience and all the curses of disobedience. The blessings begin with these words: "If you diligently obey [hearken to] the voice of the LORD your God . . . all these blessings shall come upon you" (verses 1–2). The curses begin with these words: "If you do not obey [hearken to] the voice of the LORD your God . . . all these curses will come upon you" (verse 15). The watershed is listening, or not listening, to the voice of the Lord.

I believe obedience in worship is the appointed way to come into that attitude and relationship where we really hear God's voice. Or, to state it another way, we do not hear God's voice unless we possess an attitude of worship. Then, in hearing God's voice, we enter into His rest. Thus, I believe worship is the way to rest. Only those who really know how to worship can really enjoy rest.

Look now at Hebrews 4:9–11:

> There remains, then, a Sabbath-rest for the people of God; for anyone who enters God's rest also rests from his own work, just as God did from his. Let us, therefore, make every effort to enter that rest, so that no one will fall by following their example of disobedience.
>
> NIV

Again Scripture brings out the fact that because of disobedience, the people of God failed to enter into rest. Now I am not trying to make a point here about observing the Sabbath or making Sunday the Sabbath or anything like that. I am pointing out that we can miss something important if we are not careful: God has commanded us to rest. I have come to believe that I am not pleasing God if I am busy seven days a week, every week. Furthermore, I am sure to be endangering my health. God is doing something in my heart about Sabbath-rest. I believe He can do something in your heart as well that will cause you naturally to keep His divine, eternal, unchanging laws.

Consider these questions as you meditate on this call to enter God's rest: Are you making the best of your time? Do you really know what it is to rest? Are you capable of disciplining yourself to stop doing things—even mentally? Can you ever lie down and stop thinking about what you ought to be doing?

God is more concerned with our character than with our achievements. Achievements have importance only in the realm of time. Character is eternal. It determines what we will be through eternity.

Isaiah had a vision of heaven and the glorious creatures of heaven and the throne of the Lord, which are described in Isaiah 6. He saw worship conducted in heaven and focused on creatures called seraphim. The Hebrew word *seraph* is directly related to the word for *fire*. The seraphim are the fiery creatures that are close to the throne of God. It says there that each one of them had six wings in three pairs. They were crying day and night, "Holy, holy, holy is the Lord" (verse 3). What has always impressed me is what they did with their wings: With two they covered their faces, with two they covered their feet and with two they flew (see verse 2). I interpret covering the face and feet as the humility of worship, and flying as service.

I believe in thanking God and praising Him out loud—even dancing, clapping, singing. But there comes a time when I will put my wings over my face and my wings over my feet in humble worship and listen to hear what God says.

Today, if you will hear His voice, don't harden your heart. Develop an attitude of worship and learn to rest.

Remember, the Spirit of the Lord is looking for a certain type of person—one whose heart is perfect toward God. Be that person of character, and God will show Himself strong in your behalf.

Now let's continue our "military" preparation by learning more about the One who equips and trains us for battle.

Part 2

Holy Spirit Training

9

Know Your Guide

The Spirit of the Lord.

Who is this Person who helps us through this process of character building and trains us for battle? How does He move in power in our lives? What does He teach us about Himself and His gifts?

We turn our thoughts now to the third Person of the Godhead—the Holy Spirit. It has been my experience that a better understanding of who He is can make us more effective as soldiers in God's Kingdom. It is He, after all, who continues the ministry of Jesus in our lives.

Let's start with a study of three profoundly significant adjectives that apply to the Holy Spirit: eternal, omniscient, omnipresent.

He Is Eternal

At the close of one of the first Pentecostal services I ever attended, the preacher asked me, "Do you believe that you are a sinner?" At that time I was a professional philosopher and had just completed my dissertation on "definitions" at Cambridge University. I immediately ran over in my mind various possible definitions of a "sinner." All of them applied to me exactly! So I answered, "Yes, I believe I'm a sinner!"

The preacher then asked, "Do you believe that Christ died for your sins?" I thought this over and then replied, "To tell you the truth, I can't see what the death of Jesus Christ nineteen centuries ago could have to do with the sins that I've committed in my lifetime."

The preacher was wise enough not to argue with me, but I am sure he prayed for me! A few days later I had a powerful encounter with Jesus Christ, which changed the whole course of my life. In particular, the Bible became a living, meaningful book.

Some time later I was reading in Hebrews 9:14 that "Christ . . . through *the eternal Spirit* offered Himself without spot to God" (emphasis added). Suddenly I grasped the significance of the word *eternal*. Its meaning is far broader than just something that lasts an extremely long time. It denotes something that is above and beyond the limitations of time—something that comprehends simultaneously the past, the present and the future.

When Jesus offered Himself on the cross, His sacrifice was not limited to the time at which He died. It encompassed the sins of all men of all ages—past, present and future. It included the sins that I was to commit nineteen centuries later.

The Greek adjective *eternal* has a fathomless depth of meaning. It is derived from the noun *aion*, from which we get the English word *aeon*. An *aion* is a measurement of time and occurs in a variety of expressions, as in the following literal translations (the New King James renderings are given in parentheses):

Galatians 1:5: "unto the ages of the ages" ("forever and ever")

Hebrews 7:24: "for the age" ("forever")—that is, for the duration of the present age

Jude 25: "from before every age, and now, and unto all the ages" ("both now and forever")

It is obvious that the English translations do not begin to convey the depth of the meaning of the Greek phrases. These expressions—and others like them—fill me with a sense of awe. I feel like a little drop of moisture suspended above a bottomless chasm that separates two mountains too high for me to climb. My mind cannot fully comprehend that there could be even one age made up of ages, much less that there are ages made up of such ages. Yet the eternal Holy Spirit encompasses them all, stretching from the measureless past on into the measureless future.

I begin to apprehend in a new way the title under which God is endlessly worshiped in heaven: "Lord God Almighty, who [eternally] was and is and is to come!" (Revelation 4:8).

He Is Omniscient

Closely related to the eternal nature of the Holy Spirit is His omniscience. In 1 John 3:20 the apostle confronts us with a profound yet simple revelation: *God knows all things.* There is nothing that God does not know. From the tiniest insect in the earth to the farthest star in space, there is nothing that God does not completely know. God knows things about us that we do not know about ourselves. He knows, for instance, the number of hairs that each of us has on our heads (see Matthew 10:30). He knew the number of inhabitants in the city of Nineveh (see Jonah 4:11). He knew—and controlled—the growth of the plant that shaded Jonah. He also knew—and controlled—the action of the worm that caused the plant to wither (see Jonah 4:6–7).

Paul speaks about the things that "eye has not seen, nor ear heard, nor have entered into the heart of man." Then he continues, "But God has revealed them to us through His Spirit. *For the Spirit searches all things,* yes, the deep things of God" (1 Corinthians 2:9–10, emphasis added). The Holy Spirit both plumbs the deepest depths and scales the highest heights of all that was, that is and that is to come. His knowledge is infinite.

It is in the light of this infinite knowledge that we must each be prepared to give an account of ourselves to God: "And there is no creature hidden from His sight, but all things are naked and open to the eyes of Him to whom we must give account" (Hebrews 4:13).

The supernatural knowledge and wisdom of the Holy Spirit was manifested throughout the earthly ministry of Jesus, but never do we see it more clearly than in His dealings with Judas Iscariot. When the disciples told Jesus, "We have come to believe and know that You are the Christ [Messiah], the Son of the living God" (John 6:69), Jesus' answer revealed that being the Messiah would entail being betrayed by one of His own followers: "'Did I not choose you, the twelve, and one of you is a devil?' He spoke of Judas Iscariot, the son of Simon, for it was he who would betray Him, being one of the twelve" (verses 70–71). Jesus knew by the Holy Spirit that Judas would betray Him, even before Judas knew it himself.

Even so, Judas could not carry out his plan until Jesus spoke a word that released him to do so. At the Last Supper Jesus told His disciples, "One of you will betray Me" (John 13:21). When questioned who it would be, Jesus replied,

"It is he to whom I shall give a piece of bread when I have dipped it." And having dipped the bread, He gave it to Judas Iscariot, the son of Simon. Now after the piece of bread, Satan entered him. Then Jesus said to him, "What you do, do quickly."

verses 26–27

Having received the piece of bread, Judas went out quickly—to betray Jesus.

I am awed by the realization that Judas could not carry out his plan to betray Jesus until Jesus Himself spoke the word that released him to do it. Throughout this whole scene, it was the Betrayed, not the betrayer, who was in control.

When we comprehend the completeness of God's knowledge—and in particular His foreknowledge—it gives us the assurance that no matter what happens, God is never taken by surprise. There is no such thing as an emergency in the Kingdom of heaven. And God does not merely *know* the end from the beginning, He Himself *is* both the Beginning and the End (see Revelation 21:6). And He is always in total control.

In particular, God knows those whom He has chosen to be with Him in eternity. "For whom He foreknew, He also predestined to be conformed to the image of His Son, that He might be the firstborn among many brethren" (Romans 8:29).

If, by the mercy and grace of God, we make it through to that glorious, eternal destination, Jesus will never greet anyone with the words, "I never expected to see you here!" Rather, He will say, "My child, I've been waiting for you. We couldn't sit down to the marriage feast until you came." At that glorious banquet, I believe, every place setting will carry the name of the person for whom it is prepared.

Until the number of the redeemed is complete, God waits with amazing patience, "not willing that any should perish but that all should come to repentance" (2 Peter 3:9).

He Is Omnipresent

When we say that God is *omnipresent* we mean that He is present everywhere at the same time. In Jeremiah 23:23–24, God Himself affirms this: "'Am I a God near at hand,' says the LORD, 'and not a God afar off? Can anyone hide himself in secret places, so I shall not see him?' says the LORD; 'do I not fill heaven and earth?' says the LORD."

How can this be? We know that God is seated on His throne in heaven, with Jesus at His right hand. How then can He fill heaven and earth with His presence?

David supplies the answer. First, he asks: "Where can I go *from Your Spirit*? Or where can I flee *from Your presence*?" (Psalm 139:7, emphasis added). This reveals that it is through His Spirit that God makes Himself present everywhere at the same time. Then David fills in the details:

> If I ascend into heaven, You are there;
> If I make my bed in hell, behold, You are there.
> If I take the wings of the morning,
> And dwell in the uttermost parts of the sea,
> Even there Your hand shall lead me,
> And Your right hand shall hold me.
> If I say, "Surely the darkness shall fall on me,"
> Even the night shall be light about me;
> Indeed, the darkness shall not hide from You,
> But the night shines as the day;
> The darkness and the light are both alike to You.
>
> verses 8–12

No matter where we may go, God is there by His Spirit—invisible, often imperceptible, but inescapable. For the unbeliever this may be a terrifying thought, but for the believer it is a comforting, strengthening assurance. No matter where we may find ourselves, "Even there Your hand shall lead me, and Your right hand shall hold me."

In the New Testament Jesus Himself gives us this assurance: "I will never leave you nor forsake you" (Hebrews 13:5). At times we may not be in any way conscious of His presence, but by His Holy Spirit He is there. Our surroundings may appear totally dark, but "the darkness shall not hide from [Him]."

Each one of us needs to cultivate an inner sensitivity to the Holy Spirit that does not depend on the evidence of our physical senses. When our senses tell us nothing about His presence, or even when they seem to deny it, there should be an area in the inmost depths of our own spirit that maintains an uninterrupted awareness of the Holy Spirit's presence. Then we shall more fully understand why He is given the title in John 14:26 of "the Helper" or "the Comforter" (KJV).

With this understanding of the Person of the Holy Spirit, let's look now at ways He leads us.

10

Letting the Holy Spirit Lead

One key ministry of the Holy Spirit, vital to all matters of spiritual battle, is to be our Guide. He has been sent by God the Father to lead us through life. Jesus said: "When He, the Spirit of truth, has come, He will guide you into all truth" (John 16:13). Paul explained practically how we can live as God's children: It is by being led by the Holy Spirit. "For as many as are led by the Spirit of God, these are sons of God" (Romans 8:14).

The tense used here is the continuing present tense: As many as are *regularly led* by the Spirit of God, these are sons of God. The word *son* here speaks of maturity. It is not the word for an infant, but for a grown person. Jesus makes it clear in John 3 that in order to become God's children we have to be born again of the Spirit of God. But once we have been born again, in order to grow up and become mature and complete, we need to be regularly led by the Holy Spirit.

The sad truth is that many Christians who have been born again never really go on to be led by the Holy Spirit; consequently, they never achieve maturity. They never become the kind of complete Christians that God intends. They are never fully fitted for battle. That is why it is vitally important to deal with this theme of being led by the Holy Spirit.

Achieving Righteousness

The Bible reveals two methods by which to achieve righteousness with God: law and grace—and they are mutually exclusive. If you seek to achieve righteousness by law, you cannot achieve it by grace. And if you seek to achieve righteousness by grace, then you cannot do it by keeping the law. It is extremely important to emphasize this, because it has been my observation that many Christians try to mix law and grace. They seek to keep themselves in good standing with God partly by law and partly by grace. The truth of the matter is that they do not really understand either law or grace.

Law is a set of rules that you must keep. If you keep all the rules—all the time—you achieve righteousness. *Grace*, on the other hand, is something that we cannot earn. Grace is received from God only by one way, as described in Ephesians 2:8: "For by grace you have been saved through faith."

Personally, I believe that only God Himself could conceive the method of achieving righteousness by faith. I believe that natural man, left to himself, would never have conceived such a way of achieving righteousness. To the best of my knowledge, every other major religion requires people to achieve righteousness by doing something. Different religions hold to different requirements, but, in essence, all of them think along this line: "I'll be righteous if I do *these* things and don't do *those* things."

This means that the Christian faith, if we understand it rightly, is absolutely unique. There is no other religion that even tries to offer righteousness on the basis of grace received through faith alone. But, when you embrace God's grace, He empowers you to live free from the control of sin. In Romans 6:14, Paul is speaking to people who have received the grace of God: "For sin shall not have dominion over you, for you are not under law but under grace." Notice that these two are mutually exclusive. If you are under law, you are not under grace. If you are under grace, you are not under law. You cannot be under both at the same time.

I notice also that Paul says sin will not have dominion over you because you are not under the law. The implication is that if you are under the law, sin *will* have dominion over you. If we seek to achieve righteousness by keeping the law, we will never be able to escape sin's grasp.

Let us look once more at Romans 8:14: "For as many as are led by the Spirit of God, these are sons of God." Do we live as sons of God by keeping a set of rules? No. We live as sons of God by being led by the Holy Spirit. That is the only way we can live as God's mature children.

Now let us look at Galatians 5:18: "But if you are led by the Spirit, you are not under the law." Once again, the message is clear. You become a son of God by being led by the Spirit. And if you are led by the Spirit, you are not under the law.

For many professing Christians, however, following a set of rules is like a crutch, and they limp around supporting themselves on it. God says, "Throw the crutch away and trust Me!" I have discovered that it frightens people to trust God's grace completely. We all want to hang on to a little set of rules that we keep. But it does not work! We must become completely dependent on the Holy Spirit.

God's way to righteousness and holiness is not through struggling, but through yielding—yielding to the Holy Spirit. Come to the end of your efforts and say, "Holy Spirit, take over. I cannot handle this situation—but You can!" It does not mean you do not need willpower. It means you need to use your willpower in a different way. You have to use your willpower to not do it by yourself, but to trust the Holy Spirit.

By nature, I am an independent, strong-minded person. Any time I have a problem, my natural instinct is to work out the solution for myself. It has taken me years to come to the place where I do not do that. Instead, I say, "Lord, what is Your solution?" Often, God's solution is different from anything I would ever have thought of. The Christian life is not a life of struggle; it is a life of yielding—to the Holy Spirit within us.

Paul illustrates this in Romans 7 by an example from the marriage relationship. The fruit of your life will not be determined by the amount of effort you make, but by the person to whom you are married. If you are married to your fleshly nature, you will bring forth the works of the flesh. But if—through the Holy Spirit—you are united with the resurrected Christ, through that union you will bring forth the fruit of the Spirit.

Just Stay Connected

Jesus compares our relationship with Him to a vine and its branches: "I am the true vine, and My Father is the vinedresser" (John 15:1). The vinedresser is the one who does the pruning. In verses 4 and 5, Jesus goes on to say to His disciples:

> "Abide in Me, and I in you. As the branch cannot bear fruit of itself, unless it abides in the vine, neither can you, un-

less you abide in Me. I am the vine, you are the branches. He who abides in Me, and I in him, bears much fruit; for without Me you can do nothing."

The branches of a vine do not bear grapes with a lot of effort. They do not make resolutions and say: "Now I'm going to bring forth grapes!" They bear grapes simply by being united to the trunk—the stock of the vine. The same life that is in the trunk flows through the branches, and the life in the branches brings forth the appropriate kind of fruit. Jesus said, "I am the vine, you are the branches. If you will remain related to Me—joined to Me—you'll bring forth much fruit."

Jesus goes on to talk about pruning. When a vinedresser prunes a vine, he is ruthless. He cuts the branches all the way back to the stem. You would think that vine is never going to bear fruit again. But the next year, it is more fruitful than before.

Some of our most painful struggles may be the result of bearing fruit. Right now, the Father may be pruning you. But do not give up! Do not say, "How could this happen to me?" Simply yield! Surrender to the vinedresser.

All three Persons of the Godhead are involved in this process of bringing forth fruit. The Father is the vinedresser. Jesus is the vine. And the Holy Spirit is the life that flows through the vine and into the branches. The Holy Spirit is the one who actually produces the fruit. It is not the fruit of our best efforts. It is not the fruit of religion. It is the fruit of the Holy Spirit.

A Map or a Guide?

Let me share with you a little parable to make this clear. I am sharing this out of my own experience. I know what it is to struggle to please God with my own efforts. I have tried at times to be more "religious," but I have only wound up frustrated by not knowing what to do! I have learned, however, that this is just part of the process that makes our walk with Jesus come alive.

This parable concerns a map and a guide. Suppose you need to find the way to a distant destination over country that you have never traveled. God gives you two options. You can have a map, or you can have a personal guide.

You are strong. You are clever. You are self-reliant. You respond, "I'm good at reading maps. I'll take the map." Knowing the right direction to take, you set off down the road. The sun is shining, the birds are singing and you feel happy. You say to yourself, *This is easy! This is a piece of cake!*

About three days later, you are in the middle of a jungle. It is midnight. It is raining. Hard! Furthermore, you are on the edge of a precipice. You do not know whether you are facing north, south, east or west. But a gentle voice says, "Can I help guide you?"

And you reply, "Oh, I need you! I need you!"

The Guide says, "Give me your hand, and I'll get you out of this." A little while later, you and your Guide are out on the road again and walking along side by side.

Then it occurs to you, *I was pretty silly to get so panicky just about being in that jungle. I could have made it.* So you turn around to explain this to your Guide, and the Guide is not there! You shrug your shoulders and think, *Well, I can make it on my own.* And you set off again.

About two days later, you are in the middle of a bog and you sink a little deeper with every step you take. You do not know what to do! You think to yourself, *I can't ask for help again. Last time I got it, and I didn't do the right thing.*

At this moment, you discover to your astonishment that the Guide is right beside you once more. He says, "Let me help you," and you start off together again.

At this point, you remember the map that is still in your pocket. So you take it out and offer it to the Guide saying, "Maybe you'd like that."

But the Guide says, "Thanks, I know the way, I don't need the map." Then he says, "As a matter of fact, I made the map!"

The map, of course, is the law. It is perfect. Every detail is exactly right. Every single item in the geography is correctly marked. It is up to you to decide, "I won't take the map. I'll trust my Guide."

Who is the personal Guide? The Holy Spirit, of course!

How often does this kind of thing need to happen? How many times will we go back to trusting our own wisdom and our own cleverness and in this way snub the Holy Spirit?

The Bride Who Trusted Her Guide

Genesis 24 is an account of how Abraham obtained a bride for his son Isaac. He sent his servant back to the land of Mesopotamia to find a young woman of his own family line, which—according to the culture of that time—was an essential requirement.

This story is a parable acted out in history. Abraham is a type of God the Father. Isaac is a type of Jesus Christ the Son. The chosen bride (whose name was Rebekah) is a type of the Church. Then there is one other main character who remains nameless: the servant. The servant is a type of the Holy Spirit. Genesis 24 contains the Holy Spirit's self-portrait. It is characteristic that He does not even name Himself. The Holy Spirit never draws attention to Himself, but always works to bring glory to the Father and the Son.

The servant sets off, taking with him ten camels laden with various gifts, having in mind that he is going to choose a bride. In the Middle East, whenever you make a significant choice and build a relationship, you always give a gift.

If your gift is received, you as a person are received. If your gift is rejected, then you are rejected. This is an absolutely critical part in establishing any relationship.

Having lived in that part of the world, I can tell you that camels carry an immense amount of baggage—and the servant is making the trip with no fewer than ten camels! He arrives at the place where they water the flocks and he prays: "I'm going to ask one of these young women to draw water for me. Let the one who is the chosen young woman say, 'I'll draw water for you and for your camels as well.'" (Bear in mind that a camel can drink forty gallons of water. This chosen young woman would be volunteering to draw from a well up to four hundred gallons of water.)

So here comes Rebekah, and the servant says, "Give me something to drink." Rebekah replies, "Certainly! And I'll draw for your camels as well." Then the servant says to himself, *This is the girl!* Let me add that Rebekah is a pattern of faith and works. It takes a lot of work to draw water for ten camels.

Then the servant pulls out beautiful jewels—a nose jewel and bracelets—and places them on Rebekah. The moment she accepts the jewels she is marked as the appointed bride. What would have happened if Rebekah had refused the jewels? She would never have become the bride. What can we say of a church that refuses the gifts of the Holy Spirit? It lacks the distinctive marks of the bride.

Rebekah never had a map. She had never been where the guide was taking her. She had never seen either the man she was to marry or his father. But she had a guide who knew the way. He also knew both the father and the son. He could supply her with all the information she needed.

That is how it is with you and me. We cannot make it with a map; we must have a Guide. In this life we will probably never see the Father or the Son or the place that is our destination. But if we allow the Holy Spirit to lead us, He will show us the way.

11

No Place for Hypocrisy

"And I will pray the Father, and He will give you another Helper, that He may abide with you forever—the Spirit of truth, whom the world cannot receive, because it neither sees Him nor knows Him; but you know Him, for He dwells with you and will be in you."

John 14:16–17

When Jesus promised His disciples that He would ask the Father to send them a divine Helper, He gave this Helper a special name: "the Spirit of truth." At the same time, He warned them that the world would not be able to receive this Helper.

For this, the Scripture supplies two reasons. First, from the time that men turned away from God in rebellion, they have been unwilling to accept the truth that exposes their unrighteous deeds. Because of this, they "suppress the truth in unrighteousness" (Romans 1:18).

Second, rebellion against God has exposed humanity to the domination of the god of this age, "Satan, who deceives the whole world" (Revelation 12:9). Deception is the primary weapon that Satan relies on to keep humanity under his control. Once his ability to deceive is stripped away, Satan has nothing to offer anyone except a place with him in the lake of eternal fire!

Over many centuries, human philosophy has never been able to produce a satisfactory definition of truth. On the other hand, the Bible gives a threefold answer. First, Jesus said, "*I* am . . . the truth" (John 14:6, emphasis added). Second, in praying to God the Father, He said, "*Your word* is truth" (John 17:17, emphasis added). Third, John tells us, "*The [Holy] Spirit* is truth" (1 John 5:6, emphasis added).

In the spiritual realm, therefore, there are three coordinates of truth: Jesus, the Scripture and the Holy Spirit. When these three are in agreement, we know that we have arrived at truth—absolute truth. It is important, however, that we check all three coordinates before we arrive at a conclusion. Thus, there are three questions that we must ask concerning any spiritual issue: Does it represent Jesus as He truly is? Is it in harmony with Scripture? Does the Holy Spirit bear His witness?

Historically, the Church would have been spared many errors and deceptions if it had always checked all three coordinates of truth. It is not enough that a teacher paints an appealing picture of Jesus as a perfect moral example. Or that a pastor batters his congregation with a barrage of Scripture verses. Or that an evangelist impresses his audience with a thrilling display of the supernatural. Before we can accept what is presented to us as truth, all three coordinates must be in place: Jesus, the Scripture, the Holy Spirit.

The distinctive function of the Holy Spirit, remember, is to *bear witness*: "It is the Spirit who bears witness" (1 John 5:6). The Holy Spirit bears witness to Jesus as the eternal Son of God, who shed His blood on the cross as the all-sufficient sacrifice for our sins. In the words of Charles Wesley:

> The Spirit answers to the blood
> And tells me I am born of God.

The Holy Spirit also bears witness to the truth and authority of Scripture, as Paul wrote to the Thessalonians: "For our gospel did not come to you in word only, but also in power, and *in the Holy Spirit* and in much assurance" (1 Thessalonians 1:5, emphasis added). (We will discuss the infallibility of Scripture in the next chapter.)

What Is Hypocrisy?

There can be no compromise between the Holy Spirit, who is the Spirit of truth, and Satan, who "is a liar and the father of it" (John 8:44). This was dramatically demonstrated in the early Church, when Ananias and Sapphira lied about the money that they had offered to the church. They claimed that they had brought the full price of the property they had sold, whereas in fact they had kept back part of it.

The Spirit of truth in Peter was not deceived. He charged Ananias with lying not merely to men, but also to the Holy Spirit Himself—the one who is the very Spirit of truth:

> But Peter said, "Ananias, why has Satan filled your heart to lie to the Holy Spirit and keep back part of the price of the land for yourself? While it remained, was it not your own? And after it was sold, was it not in your own control? Why have you conceived this thing in your heart? You have not lied to men but to God." Then Ananias, hearing these words, fell down and breathed his last. So great fear came upon all those who heard these things.
>
> Acts 5:3–5

Three hours later Sapphira came in and repeated the same lie. Like her husband, she paid for it with her life.

Rightly defined, the sin of which Ananias and Sapphira were guilty was *hypocrisy*—religious pretense. They were pretending to be more generous and more committed to the Lord than they really were. Jesus reserved His strongest words of condemnation for this sin in the religious leaders of His day. Seven times in Matthew 23 He said to them: "Woe to you . . . hypocrites!"

Our English words *hypocrite* and *hypocrisy* are derived directly from the Greek word *hupokrites*, which means "actor." This is the essence of hypocrisy: putting on a religious act. Probably no sin is more common among religious people than hypocrisy. In fact, some forms of religion almost demand it.

When people enter a religious building, their whole demeanor changes. They are no longer natural, free and open. They appear to be gripped by some kind of invisible "cramp." They feel required to put on a religious mask. Different branches of religion may require masks of different kinds, but few of them allow people to be their real selves.

When the preacher condemns certain sins, these people respond with a dutiful "Amen!" But outside the church they commit those same sins without even a twinge of conscience. If they pray out loud, they use a special tone of voice and often a special vocabulary. They do not stop to consider how a human father would feel if his child were to address him with such artificial language or to put on an unnatural form of behavior just to impress him.

The God of the Bible has no time for hypocrites. This comes out clearly in the story of Job. Job's three friends poured forth a torrent of religious platitudes. They said, in effect, "God always blesses the righteous; they never suffer unjustly." And: "God always judges the wicked; they never

93

prosper." Yet the facts of history demonstrate that this is not true. It is just religious talk!

Job, on the other hand, was completely frank. He said, in effect, "God is not treating me fairly. I have done nothing to deserve all this. But even if He kills me, I will still trust Him."

I quoted Job 42:7 in an earlier chapter—the Lord revealing His estimate of the conduct of Job and his friends. Look at it again in this light: "The LORD said to Eliphaz the Temanite, 'My wrath is aroused against you and your two friends, for you have not spoken of Me what is right, as My servant Job has.'"

We need to ask ourselves: How does this kind of religious behavior differ from the sin of Ananias and Sapphira, which cost them their lives?

The Moment of Truth

In this light, let's recall the fact that King David was guilty of two terrible sins. First, he committed adultery with Bathsheba, the wife of his neighbor Uriah. Then, to cover up his sin, he procured the murder of Uriah.

Apparently David got away with all this. He still went through his regular forms of worship. He still carried out his duties as king. He still lived in the royal palace. Outwardly nothing had changed—until God's messenger, the prophet Nathan, confronted David with his sin. At that moment David's eternal destiny hung in the balance. By the grace of God, David made the right response. He offered no excuses, made no attempt to cover up. He acknowledged, "I have sinned." (See 2 Samuel 12:1–15.)

Later on, we read in Psalm 51 that David offered up a prayer of confession and then a cry for mercy. Verses 5 and

6 each begin with the word *Behold,* expressing a sudden revelation of a vital truth.

Verse 5 says: "Behold, I was brought forth in iniquity, and in sin my mother conceived me." David had come face-to-face with something that only the Spirit of truth can reveal: not just the sinful acts that he had committed, but the awful, evil power of inherited sinfulness that indwells every descendant of Adam.

Verse 6 reveals the only basis on which God offers deliverance from the power of indwelling sin: "Behold, You desire *truth in the inward parts*" (emphasis added). After his sin, David had continued to go through all the outward forms of behavior appropriate to his role as king. But now there was a vast gap between his outward behavior and the inward condition of his heart. He had become a hypocrite—an actor playing a part which no longer corresponded to what was in his heart. For this there was only one remedy: honest confession and wholehearted repentance.

From Palm Sunday to Good Friday

This truth runs through the whole Bible: *God will never compromise with sin.* This is illustrated dramatically by two days in the life of Jesus: Palm Sunday and Good Friday.

On Palm Sunday, Jesus entered Jerusalem as a popular hero—"the prophet from Nazareth of Galilee" (Matthew 21:11). The whole city was open to Him. He could easily have moved aside His bitter enemies, the religious leaders, and established Himself as King. That was what the people were longing for.

Yet He chose another way. Five days later He hung rejected and naked on a cruel cross. Why? Because God will never compromise with sin and the only way to deal with sin was the sacrifice of Jesus on the cross.

Many Christians today are speaking and praying about "revival." They often overlook the fact that there is one barrier to revival that can never be bypassed. It is *sin*. Until sin is dealt with, true revival can never come. And there is only one way to deal with sin: "He who covers his sins will not prosper, but whoever confesses and forsakes them will have mercy" (Proverbs 28:13).

Frankly stated, many sections of the contemporary Church are full of "covered sin." Here are some sins that Christians often seek to cover:

1. Abuse of a child—physical, emotional, sexual—or a combination
2. Broken marriage vows
3. Unethical dealing with money
4. Addiction to pornography (I have been shocked to discover how common this is among leaders in the Church)
5. Gluttony—overindulgence of our physical appetites

God's remedy is twofold: First, *confess*; then, *forsake*. It is seldom easy to confess our sins. Yet there is no other remedy. "If we confess our sins, He is faithful and just to forgive us our sins and to cleanse us from all unrighteousness" (1 John 1:9). God has never committed Himself to forgive sins that we are not willing to confess.

But it is not enough merely to confess. We must also "forsake." We must make a resolute determination not to continue to commit the sin we have confessed. We must follow the succinct advice that Daniel gave to King Nebuchadnezzar: "Break off thy sins by righteousness" (Daniel 4:27, KJV). Between righteousness and sin there is no middle ground. "All unrighteousness is sin" (1 John 5:17). Whatever is not righteous is sinful.

Are you face-to-face with a difficult decision?

If this chapter has caused you to question things in your life that you have been accepting, or has confronted you with some area of disobedience, open up to the Spirit of truth! He is ready and willing to help you.

12

The Holy Spirit
and the Word

When you consult a physician, you want to have the assurance that she knows what she's talking about. We expect doctors to be able to tell us how to prevent disease, remedy pain or sickness when necessary, and stay healthy and fit. We want them to have plenty of experience in the field, but they also need to have taken the appropriate training. How many of us would see a doctor who had never been to medical school, never studied the books and had not stayed abreast of advances in research? How equipped would that person be to help others?

The same applies to us as Christians preparing for spiritual battle. We can have all the "field experience" imaginable, we work hard to grow in character, but if we have not studied The Book—if we are not relying on the authoritative manual—we will not be successful. We can espouse reasonable philosophy and noble thoughts about God all day long, but if we are not rooted in *His* Word, *our* words are not reliable. There is no way around it: We cannot hope to endure if our Christian lives are not built on the foundation of the Word of God.

There are two applications in Scripture of the title "the Word of God." One is to the Bible itself (God's written Word), and the other is to Jesus Christ (God's personal Word). Each of them is called the Word of God. If we want to be rightly related to Jesus, we must be rightly related to the Bible. So let's discover the authority and the power of God's Word and how the Holy Spirit bears witness to its truth.

Whose Word Is It?

The word *authority* comes from the word *author*. The authority of any work is the authority of the author. In other words, it is the author who gives authority to whatever he produces. So it is important to know the identity of the author of the Bible.

> All Scripture is given by inspiration of God, and is profitable for doctrine, for reproof, for correction, for instruction in righteousness, that the man of God may be complete, thoroughly equipped for every good work.
>
> 2 Timothy 3:16–17

If you want to be complete and thoroughly equipped for every good work, the source of it all is Scripture. Paul also says that "all Scripture is given by inspiration of God." The Greek word for "inspiration of God" is defined as "God-breathed." The word for "breath" and the word for "spirit" are identical. Paul is saying, "All Scripture is inbreathed by the Spirit of God." The authority behind all Scripture is the authority of the Holy Spirit. He is ultimately the author. He used many different instruments, but the authority of the Holy Spirit—who is God Himself—directed each one. When we draw from Scripture, we are drawing from the authority of God Himself.

Paul also notes that *all* Scripture is inspired, not some. We do not have the luxury of separating the passages we consider valuable from those we consider less valuable. The Holy Spirit Himself has declared *all* Scripture to be inspired by God and *all* Scripture to be profitable. There are no books or chapters or verses that we can leave out or deem unimportant. Let's not just focus on a few well-known passages of Scripture and think that they are all that matter. We will find that we move from strength to strength as we meditate on, study and apply the Word of God. Jesus said we need to be hearing and doing the Word of God; not just hearing, but hearing and doing.

Someone might say, "But the men who wrote the Bible were in many cases very weak and fallible. The Bible even records a lot of their sins!" And that would be correct. I believe that is a mark of the Bible's accuracy—that it records the sins of the people who wrote it. A lot of people today would omit their sins and try to present themselves as infallible. The Bible's writers do not. We have seen how David, who wrote most of the psalms, recorded his serious sins for all to read.

So how can the Bible be infallible if the people who wrote it were fallible? There is a beautiful answer given to that question in one simple verse: "The words of the LORD are pure words, like silver tried in a furnace of earth, purified seven times" (Psalm 12:6).

This is a picture of how people used to purify metal. They built a furnace of clay, lit a fire in it and then put the metal there to be purified. So we can draw this analogy: The *furnace of clay* is the human instrument, just clay; the *fire* is the Holy Spirit; and He purifies the *silver*, which is the message. This tells us how fallible men and women can be the channels to produce an inspired and an authoritative Word of God. The clay is the human vessel, the fire is the Holy Spirit and the silver—purified seven times, absolutely pure—is the message of God.

The Bible, though it came through vessels of clay—weak, fallible, sinful men and women—has been purified seven times by the fire of the Holy Spirit. It is totally reliable.

Jesus and the Word

We need to consider the attitude of Jesus Himself toward the Bible, because for us who are His disciples, He is the pattern. How did He relate to the written Word? Let's begin with His teaching on the Scriptures of His day, what we call the Old Testament.

In a discussion one day with Jewish leaders, Jesus said this: "If He called them gods, to whom the word of God came (and the Scripture cannot be broken) . . ." (John 10:35). Jesus here gave the Bible the two titles that His followers have used ever since: *the word of God* and *the Scripture*. His use of "the word of God" means it proceeds from God. It did not proceed from man; it came from heaven, from God. And His use of "the Scripture" means that which has been recorded in writing. God has said many things that are not recorded in writing, but those that are recorded in the Bible are there for our special benefit. They contain everything we need to know for our salvation.

Jesus' attitude is summed up in the next words of that verse: "The Scripture cannot be broken." Nothing can express the authority of Scripture more completely than that simple phrase. We receive further affirmation in these next verses from the book of Matthew, in which Jesus speaks of the Old Testament:

"Do not think that I came to destroy the Law or the Prophets. I did not come to destroy but to fulfill. For assuredly, I say to you, till heaven and earth pass away, one jot or one tittle will by no means pass from the law till all is fulfilled."

Matthew 5:17–18

The word *jot*, in modern Hebrew, is *yod*, the smallest letter in the alphabet. *Tittle* (*keraia*) is a little curve put on a letter to distinguish it from a similar letter. Those are the two smallest items in written Hebrew text, and Jesus said that not one of them used in Scripture will ever pass away. He was not talking about the spoken Word of God at that point, because the words *jot* and *tittle* only apply to that which is in writing. We see from this that Jesus endorsed the total authority of the written Word of God.

A little further on, quite near the end of His ministry, Jesus was dealing with the Sadducees who were the liberals of that day, the people who did not accept the authority of all Scripture. In fact, they only accepted the authority of the first five books, the Pentateuch. They were challenging the teaching that there will be a resurrection of the dead, and they came to Jesus with a carefully designed question. This is how Jesus answered them:

"But concerning the resurrection of the dead, have you not read what was spoken to you by God, saying, 'I am the God of Abraham, the God of Isaac, and the God of Jacob'? God is not the God of the dead, but of the living."

Matthew 22:31–32

Notice how Jesus applied that Scripture. These words were written by Moses fourteen centuries earlier—they were actually words spoken by the Lord directly to Moses. But Jesus did not refer to them as something that was applicable only to Moses fourteen centuries before. He said, "Have you not read what was spoken to you by God?" The Scripture is never out of date. It is never just the record of human cleverness. It is God-inspired. And even if it was written three thousand years ago, it is still God speaking to you and me today. That is the authority of Scripture as Jesus understood it.

Holy Spirit Authority

We have Jesus' own words about the Old Testament, but what about the New Testament? The authority behind the New Testament is the same that is behind the Old Testament. In the verses below Jesus is preparing His disciples for the fact that He is going to leave.

> "These things I have spoken to you while being present with you. But the Helper, the Holy Spirit, whom the Father will send in My name, He will teach you all things, and bring to your remembrance all things that I said to you."
>
> John 14:25–26

The authority behind the writings of the apostles is the authority of the Holy Spirit. And Jesus said that the Holy Spirit would do two things: "Whatever I didn't teach you, He will teach you; and whatever I said that you might have forgotten, He will bring to your remembrance." So the record of the gospels does not depend on human memory; it depends on the truth of the Holy Spirit.

Incidentally, let me point out that Jesus breaks the laws of grammar to emphasize that the Holy Spirit is not an "it" but a "He." According to Greek grammar, He should have used the preposition *it*, but He did not; He said *He*. This is vitally important to understand: The Holy Spirit is not just an *it*, He is a *He*, a Person, and we need to relate to Him as a Person.

In John 16, Jesus reveals another important characteristic of the Holy Spirit: "He will not speak on His own authority, but whatever He hears He will speak; and He will tell you things to come. He will glorify Me, for He will take of what is Mine and declare it to you" (John 16:13–14).

The Holy Spirit always glorifies Jesus. If you ever are confronted by spiritual manifestations that do not glorify Jesus but give glory to a person or in some other direction, you can be sure that it is not the Holy Spirit. The supreme ministry of the Holy Spirit is to reveal and to glorify Jesus. The Bible says we are to test the spirits, and you can test if a thing is from the Holy Spirit if it glorifies Jesus. If it does not—even though it may sound good or spiritual or may be uttered in a loud, resounding voice—it is not from the Holy Spirit, because He will not glorify anyone but Jesus. I am very conscious of that myself. I continually examine myself by asking, "Am I giving the glory to Jesus, or am I trying to persuade people that Derek Prince is someone important?" Derek Prince is just a sinner saved by the grace of God.

Relying on the Word Today

The Bible gives us examples of how Jesus used the authority of Scripture in His life—examples that we can follow. The story of Jesus in the wilderness being tempted by Satan is a powerful one. Just before this story begins, the third chapter of Matthew records how Jesus was baptized in the Jordan:

> After his baptism, as Jesus came up out of the water, the heavens were opened and he saw the Spirit of God descending like a dove and settling on him. And a voice from heaven said, "This is my beloved Son, and I am fully pleased with him."
>
> Matthew 3:16–17, NLT

You and I might think that, after this, Jesus was set to have an easy time. He had the endorsement of both the Father and the Spirit—along with that of the prophet John the Baptist. But that was not to be.

After this serene and powerful encounter, Jesus found Himself in the wilderness fasting for forty days and being tempted by Satan. Please do not imagine that God's blessing will always make life easy for you. In fact, in a certain sense, it may make life more difficult, because Satan much more strongly opposes those whom God has anointed.

Luke says that Jesus was led by the Spirit into the wilderness (see Luke 4:1), but at the end of the forty days, He came out in the power of the Holy Spirit (see verse 14). Note the distinction. It is one thing to be led by the Spirit; it is another thing to move and operate in the power of the Spirit. Jesus did not do the latter until He had His conflict with Satan and won. In some degree or other, each of us will need to walk that same path. We will have to overcome temptation and opposition in order to move in the power of the Holy Spirit.

When Satan came to Jesus, the first thing he tempted Jesus to do was to doubt. That is nearly always the initial approach of Satan. He will not immediately deny the Word of God; he will question it or cause you to doubt it. "Now when the tempter came to Him, he said, 'If You are the Son of God, command that these stones become bread'" (Matthew 4:3, NASB).

God had just spoken from heaven, saying, "This is My beloved Son." Satan was challenging Jesus to doubt what He had heard from God. "If You are the Son of God, then do something to prove it. Make these stones bread."

Here is Jesus' response: "But He answered and said, 'It is written, "Man shall not live on bread alone, but on every word that proceeds out of the mouth of God"'" (Matthew 4:4, NASB). He relied on the full and unbreakable authority of the written Word of God. Each time Jesus was tempted,

He responded with, "It is written." And whenever Jesus said that, Satan changed the subject. He knew he had no answer to the Scripture.

This gives us two very important directives. One, we must rely on the full authority of Scripture, and, two, we must use it to deal with temptation.

We will learn more about battle techniques later, but I want to close this chapter on Holy Spirit-inspired Scripture with this point: Don't ever think that you are clever enough to argue with the devil; he is much more clever than you are. He has been in this business a long, long time. Don't try to convince him with your arguments. Instead, meet him with the Scripture. The Scripture is authoritative. Accept it. Live by it. Answer the devil with it.

But remember, you have to speak it. In Ephesians 6:17, Paul says, "And take . . . the sword of the Spirit, which is the word of God." There are two Greek words for *word*: one is *logos*, the other is *rhema*. *Logos* is the total, eternal counsel of God. *Rhema* is a spoken word of God. This is the word used in Ephesians 6:17. Paul says to take "the sword of the Spirit, which is the [*rhema*, the spoken] word of God."

The Bible will not protect you if it is just sitting on your bookshelf, or even if it is on your bedside table. It only works when you quote it. You have to take it in your mouth and say it for yourself. Then it becomes a sharp sword from which the devil backs off. He has no answer for it.

13

Taking Up the Spiritual Gifts

W e saw in chapter 10 that the story of Abraham's servant and the young woman Rebekah offers a historical analogy of the relationship between the Holy Spirit and the Church. If we look further, we see that the analogy reveals a remarkable desire of the Holy Spirit.

When the servant found the young woman who was to become Isaac's bride, his first act was to place on her face a conspicuous nose jewel. By accepting the gift, Rebecca committed herself to become Isaac's bride. Had she refused the gift, she would have rejected and dishonored Isaac. She could never have become his bride.

Today, in a similar way, God has sent His Holy Spirit with abundant provision for the bride of His Son, Jesus—the Church. Included in it are nine beautiful spiritual gifts. By accepting these gifts, the Church is marked out as the one who is committed to become the Bride of Christ.

Nine Supernatural Gifts

These nine gifts are listed in 1 Corinthians 12:8–10. To bring out the exact meaning, I give the following literal translation:

1. A word of wisdom
2. A word of knowledge
3. Faith
4. Gifts of healings
5. Working of miracles (literally, powers)
6. Prophecy
7. Discernings of spirits
8. Kinds of tongues
9. Interpretation of tongues

All these gifts are "manifestations." The Holy Spirit Himself is invisible, but through these gifts He manifests Himself. He impacts our senses in ways that we can see or hear or feel.

All of them are "for the profit of all." Through them Christians can minister to one another. The gifts all serve some practical purpose. They are tools, not toys.

All these gifts are supernatural. They are not the product of natural ability or special education. An illiterate person may receive a word of wisdom or of knowledge. Similarly, the gift of "faith" goes beyond the faith that we all need for salvation. It is also distinct from the fruit of faith, which comes by a process of natural growth. It is a supernatural faith that goes beyond our natural ability and produces supernatural results.

It is often suggested that these gifts were withdrawn at the close of the apostolic age and are not available today. Paul, however, thanked God for the Christians at Corinth because "you do not lack any spiritual gift as you eagerly wait for our Lord Jesus Christ to be revealed" (1 Corinthians 1:7, NIV). Obviously, therefore, Christians are expected to continue to exercise spiritual gifts until the return of Christ.

The first two gifts that Paul lists—a word of wisdom and a word of knowledge—are related in a practical way. A word of knowledge gives us the facts about a situation. Then a word of wisdom shows us how God wants us to deal with that situation.

Some of the gifts are plural in both parts: for example, gifts of healings, working of miracles, discernings of spirits, kinds of tongues. This indicates that each healing, each miracle, each discerning, each utterance in a certain tongue (language) is a gift. If a certain gift regularly manifests itself through a certain person, we may say that the person has that gift.

Gifts That Cannot Be Earned

It must be emphasized that all these are gifts of God's grace. They are received by faith. We can never earn them. We can never be "good enough" to exercise them.

In 1941 in the middle of the night I had a powerful, life-changing encounter with Jesus Christ in a barrack room of the British Army. About a week later, in the same barrack room, I spoke for the first time in an unknown tongue. Then—quite unexpectedly—I went on to speak out the "interpretation" in beautiful, poetic English. It was an outline of God's plan for my life and ministry, which has been fulfilled—stage by stage—up to the present time.

Fortunately for me, I was too "unspiritual" to know that you had to go to church to get saved, or that after speaking in a tongue you had to wait six months to receive the gift of interpretation!

From 1957 to 1961 I served as principal of a teacher training college for African teachers in Kenya. During that time we had a sovereign visitation of the Holy Spirit in our college. In meetings with my students I saw all nine gifts of the Spirit in operation among us at various times. I also saw two of my students—on different occasions—raised from the dead. They both testified later of what they had experienced while their spirits were out of their bodies.

Later, in America, I received an unexpected "gift" for ministering to people who were lame. As I seated them in a chair and held their feet in my hands, the shorter leg would grow out in front of my eyes and they would be healed. Some people, however, suggested that this was not an appropriate ministry for a dignified, scholarly Bible teacher. I decided to ask the Lord about this and I felt He gave me this answer: *I have given you a gift. There are two things you can do with it. You can use it and get more. Or you can fail to use it and lose it.* There and then I decided to go on using what God had given me, and indeed I did receive more.

On occasion I have seen a short leg grow out as much as two inches. Also the release of God's supernatural power in this way triggered other miracles. In one place, without any special prayer being offered, a man was healed of three major infirmities and delivered from nicotine addiction.

I remember one woman who came with a paper bag in her hand and a one-and-a-half-inch buildup on the heel of one shoe. When I took her feet in my hands, her short leg grew out one and a half inches. Then she opened her paper bag and took out a pair of new shoes with normal heels. They fitted her perfectly.

I eventually decided that the scriptural name for my gift was "working of miracles (power)."

About the same time God directed me into what I came to see as a different application of the same gift. He began to use me in the public casting out of demons. Once again, there were those who objected to the noisy and disorderly manifestations that often accompanied this ministry. I observed in the gospels, however, that similar manifestations often accompanied the ministry of Jesus and so I decided to continue. In the years that have followed I have seen thousands of people wonderfully delivered from demon power.

If we desire the unhindered operation of spiritual gifts, we sometimes need to set ourselves free from traditional ideas of how we should behave "in church."

Another key to exercising spiritual gifts is to cultivate sensitivity to the Holy Spirit and to make room for Him to move as and when He wills. On one occasion, Ruth and I were having lunch with a Christian couple, and the wife shared that she had a medically diagnosed genetic defect that made her unable to utilize certain amino acids. Her brain was progressively deteriorating.

The husband left to keep another appointment, and we walked back with the wife to their apartment. On the parking lot we paused for a moment to say good-bye. Prompted by the Holy Spirit, Ruth said, "Let me pray for you." Then we parted.

About three weeks later the husband told us that his wife had been completely healed. This was later confirmed at the same hospital where her condition had been diagnosed.

In that instance, God had just one place and one moment where He made healing available. Because Ruth responded to the prompting of the Holy Spirit, healing came and God was glorified.

Limitations of Spiritual Gifts

I feel a familiar tingle of excitement as I think back over some of the ways in which I have seen spiritual gifts manifested. At the same time, however, it is important to understand that there are definite limits to what we can expect from spiritual gifts.

First of all, spiritual gifts are limited to the present life. Speaking of the gifts of prophecy, tongues and the word of knowledge, Paul says,

> But where there are prophecies, they will cease; where there are tongues, they will be stilled; where there is knowledge, it will pass away. For we know in part and we prophesy in part, but when perfection comes, the imperfect disappears.
>
> 1 Corinthians 13:8–10, NIV

We are still living in the "imperfect" age. But when we pass from time to eternity and then put on our resurrection bodies, we will no longer need the fragmentary blessings that come to us through tongues or prophecy or a word of knowledge. The same applies to other gifts such as healings or miracles. Our resurrection bodies will never need them!

If people are excessively preoccupied with spiritual gifts, it often indicates that they are more concerned with the things of time than eternity. Such people need to heed Paul's warning: "If only for this life we have hope in Christ, we are to be pitied more than all men" (1 Corinthians 15:19, NIV).

More important still, the exercise of spiritual gifts gives no indication of a person's character. Let me illustrate with a crude example. Suppose a person who is lazy, deceitful and conceited receives an unearned gift of one million dollars. His character will not be changed at all. He will still be lazy, deceitful, conceited. In fact, he may even be more conceited because he has a million dollars in his bank account!

The same applies to a person who receives a dramatic spiritual gift, such as prophecy or healings or miracles. If he was weak and unstable before, he will be just as weak and unstable afterward. But his new gift will give him greater influence with people, and he will have the added responsibility of exercising it in a way that is righteous and pleasing to God.

A major problem in the charismatic renewal is that people tend to assess ministers more by their gifts than by their character. Yet experience has demonstrated time and time again that it is possible for a person to exercise dramatic, impressive gifts and yet have a very defective character. Sometimes such people may even use their gifts to cover up the imperfections of their characters.

There was a minister in a Scandinavian country who preached on the "latter rain" of the Holy Spirit in such a powerful way that people in his congregation actually felt the Holy Spirit falling on them like drops of rain. Yet he went straight out from those services to commit adultery. When he was charged with this, people could not believe that a man who preached like that would commit such a sin—until eventually he acknowledged it himself.

As a young preacher, I greatly admired an older man who had a spectacular ministry of miracles. He also taught forcefully that it is possible for a Christian to live without ever sinning. Yet eventually he divorced his wife, married his secretary and died an alcoholic. Other well-known and successful preachers have experienced similar personal tragedies.

When confronted with cases such as these, people often respond, "But surely if a person misuses one of these gifts, God would take it away!"

Yet the answer is no! The gifts of the Spirit are exactly what the name implies—genuine gifts, not loans with conditions attached or a repayment schedule. "For the gifts and the calling of God are irrevocable" (Romans 11:29). Once we receive one of these gifts, we are free to use it, misuse it or just not use it at all. Ultimately, however, God will require an account of what we have done—or not done.

We need always to bear in mind the warning of Jesus: "You will know them *by their fruits*" (Matthew 7:20, NASB, emphasis added)—not by their gifts. Jesus followed up these words by an explicit warning that the exercise of spiritual gifts is not necessarily a passport to heaven:

> "Not everyone who says to Me, 'Lord, Lord,' shall enter the kingdom of heaven, but he who does the will of My Father in heaven. Many will say to Me in that day, 'Lord, Lord, have we not prophesied in Your name, cast out demons in Your name, and done many wonders in Your name?' And then I will declare to them, 'I never knew you; depart from Me, you who practice lawlessness!'"
>
> Matthew 7:21–23

This indicates that it is possible for a person to exercise spiritual gifts and at the same time to "practice lawlessness." What is "lawlessness"? It is an arrogant assumption that God's moral and ethical standards no longer apply to those who can exercise gifts of supernatural power.

Obviously, such ministries may at times confront us with the need to make difficult personal decisions. How should we respond?

First of all, we must keep in mind Paul's warning to Timothy: "Do not . . . share in other people's sins; keep yourself pure" (1 Timothy 5:22).

Second, we must also keep in mind the warning that Jesus gave us concerning such unethical ministries: "Heaven is for those who do the will of My Father in heaven." We each need to ask ourselves: What is the will of God in my life? What does my Father expect of me?

For my part, I feel that God has given me a clear, simple answer: "God wants you to be holy" (1 Thessalonians 4:3, NLT; see also NIV). To this the Holy Spirit has added a warning: "Without holiness no one will see the Lord" (Hebrews 12:14, NIV). It is my determination to "pursue holiness."

Now let's look at the opposite side of the coin: the fruit of the Holy Spirit.

14

Developing Spiritual Fruit

There is a difference in kind between gifts and fruit. This may be illustrated by comparing a Christmas tree with an apple tree.

Put simply, we might say that a Christmas tree offers gifts freely. No time or effort is required of the persons receiving the gifts.

Both time and effort, however, are required to cultivate the fruit that comes from an apple tree. First, the seed must be placed in the earth. From this a root goes down into the soil and at the same time a sprout rises upward. Over a period of years the sprout grows into a tree. In due course blossoms appear on the tree. Then these fall off and fruit begins to develop.

If the tree is to become strong, the blossoms or the young fruit must be plucked off in the first years so that the tree's root system will develop to support a strong tree. Several years must pass before the apples are fit to eat. (Under

the Law of Moses at least four years were required. See
Leviticus 19:23–25.)

At various stages in its growth an apple tree is fragile.
Strong winds may uproot the young tree, or at a later stage
frost may destroy either the blossoms or the fruit.

In this process seed and fruit are linked to each other
inseparably. Fruit must grow from a seed, but it takes fruit
to produce further seeds. At the beginning of creation God
ordained that every fruit tree should yield fruit "according
to its kind . . . whose seed is in itself" (Genesis 1:12).

Forms of Spiritual Fruit

The New Testament speaks of spiritual *gifts* in the plural.
As we saw in the last chapter, the nine gifts are listed in
1 Corinthians 12:8–10. The New Testament speaks of spiritual
fruit in the singular. The nine forms of spiritual fruit are listed
in Galatians 5:22–23: love, joy, peace, longsuffering (patience),
kindness, goodness, faithfulness, gentleness, self-control.

Love—the primary form of fruit—is listed first. The others that follow may be understood as different ways in
which the fruit of love manifests itself.

Joy is love rejoicing
Peace is love resting
Longsuffering is love forbearing
Kindness is love serving others
Goodness is love seeking the best for others
Faithfulness is love keeping its promises
Gentleness is love ministering to the hurts of others
Self-control is love in control

We could also describe the fruit of the Spirit as different
ways in which the character of Jesus manifests itself through

those whom He indwells. When all the forms of fruit are fully developed, it is as if Jesus by the Holy Spirit is incarnated in His disciples. Like the apple tree, this fruit grows in stages. It is these stages that I want us to focus on.

The Seven Stages of Growth

Peter lists these stages, but begins by warning us that to go through this process successfully will demand *diligence*. Paul expresses the same thing in another way when he says, "The *hard-working* farmer must be first to partake of the crops" (2 Timothy 2:6, emphasis added). There can be no real success in developing Christian character without diligence or hard work.

When the seed of God's Word is implanted in the heart, faith starts to grow. This is the indispensable starting point of the process. Then out of faith there follow seven stages of development until the Christian character is fully formed Christian character. Peter lists these successive stages in 2 Peter 1:5–7. I have noted them in italics below:

> But also for this very reason, giving all diligence, add to your faith *virtue*, to virtue *knowledge*, to knowledge *self-control*, to self-control *perseverance*, to perseverance *godliness*, to godliness *brotherly kindness*, and to brotherly kindness *love*.

Stage one is variously translated *virtue* (NKJV) or *moral excellence* (NASB). Originally, in secular Greek, the word was applied to excellence in any area of life—to molding a clay pot, steering a boat or playing a flute. Here in the New Testament also, I believe, its meaning should not be restricted solely to moral character. It covers every possible area of life.

A teacher who comes to Christ should become an *excellent* teacher. A nurse should become an *excellent* nurse. A

Christian businessman or woman should excel in his or her field of business. There is no room for sloppiness or laziness in any area of the Christian life. Very rarely, if ever, does God call a person out of failure in a secular calling to success in a spiritual calling. He who is unfaithful in the least (the secular) will be unfaithful also in the greatest (the spiritual) (see Luke 16:10).

Stage two of spiritual development is *knowledge*. There are, of course, many different forms of knowledge. The knowledge extolled in Scripture is primarily practical, not merely theoretical. It is knowledge that *works*. Since I came to Christ out of a background of speculative philosophy, this was what impressed me most about the Bible. It was so intensely practical!

The scriptural example is the teaching of Jesus Himself. It does not come under the category of what we would call "theology." He never propounded complicated, abstract theories. His teaching was based on familiar, practical activities: sowing seed, catching fish, caring for livestock.

The most essential form of knowledge in the Christian life is the knowledge of God's will as revealed in Scripture. This, too, is practical. It demands a regular, systematic study of the whole Bible.

> All Scripture is given by inspiration of God, and is profitable for doctrine, for reproof, for correction, for instruction in righteousness, that the man of God may be complete, thoroughly equipped for every good work.
>
> Timothy 3:16–17

I have been shocked to discover how many people who claim to be serious Christians have never once read through the entire Bible. Such people set limits of their own making to their spiritual development.

After knowledge comes stage three: *self-control*—also called *self-discipline* (see 2 Timothy 1:7, NIV). This is the stage at which a Christian must prove himself a genuine *disciple*—that is, a person under *discipline*—and not a mere church member. This kind of discipline must be applied in every major area of our personalities—our emotions, our attitudes, our appetites, our thought lives. It must govern not only our actions, but—more importantly—our reactions.

Until we have developed this kind of discipline, we cannot move up to the fourth stage, *perseverance*, which implies the ability to overcome the various tests and trials that will inevitably expose any weak, undisciplined areas of our personality. That pinpoints one major reason why some Christians never progress beyond a certain stage of spiritual development. They never fulfill these two requirements of *self-control* and *endurance*. To take another illustration from the apple tree, their blossoms are blown away by the winds of adversity or their young fruit is killed by the frost of rejection.

In the three remaining stages of development, the beauty of a truly Christian character unfolds. *Godliness*, the fifth stage, is the mark of a person whose life is centered in God—a person who has become a vessel of the presence of God. Wherever such a person goes, the atmosphere is permeated by a faint, but unique and pervasive fragrance. There may not be any preaching or other religious activity. Yet people become strangely aware of eternal issues.

Smith Wigglesworth related an incident that illustrates the impact that a godly presence can have in a nonreligious atmosphere. After some moments of private prayer, Smith took his seat in a railway carriage. Without a word spoken, the man in the opposite seat—a complete stranger—blurted out, "Your presence convicts me of sin." Smith was then able to introduce him to Christ.

The last two stages of development depict two different kinds of love. The first, *brotherly kindness*, describes the way that believers in Jesus Christ should relate to their fellow believers—that is, their brothers and sisters in the Lord.

When I first began to consider this list of the seven stages of spiritual development, it surprised me that "brotherly kindness"—the kind of love that Christians should have for one another—should be the next to the last stage. But then I realized that the Bible is realistic. It does not paint a sentimental, religious picture of the way that we, as Christians, relate to one another. Let me say something that may shock you: *It is not easy for Christians to love one another.*

This is amply confirmed by two thousand years of Church history. Scarcely a century has passed that has not been marked by bitter strife and contention—and even open hatred—between rival groups of Christians, all of whom often claimed to be "the true Church."

The fact that a person has repented of his sins and claimed salvation in Christ does not mean that his whole character has been instantly transformed. Certainly a vitally important process of change has been set in motion, but it may take many years for that change to be worked out in every area of a person's character.

When David needed smooth stones to fit in his sling to slay Goliath, he went down to the valley—the lowly place of humility. There in the brook he found the kind of stones he needed (see 1 Samuel 17:40). What had made them smooth? Two pressures: first, the water flowing over them; second, their continual jostling against one another.

That is a picture of how Christian character is formed. First, there is the continual "washing of water by the word" (Ephesians 5:26). Second, as the stones jostle one another in personal relationships, the rough edges are gradually worn down, until they become "smooth."

In parentheses, let me add that when Jesus needs "living stones" for His sling, He, too, goes to the valley—the place of humility. There He chooses stones that have been made "smooth" by the action of God's Word and by the pressures of regular fellowship with other believers. It is a mark of spiritual maturity to sincerely love our fellow

Christians, not simply for what they are in themselves, but for what they mean to Jesus, who shed His lifeblood for each of them.

The final stage of development—*agape love*—represents the full, ripe fruit of Christian character. This is no longer how we relate only to our fellow believers. It is God's own love for the unthankful and the unholy. It is the love that causes us to "bless those who curse [us], do good to those who hate [us], and pray for those who spitefully use [us] and persecute [us]" (Matthew 5:44).

It is the love that Christ demonstrated on the cross when He prayed for those who crucified Him, "Father, forgive them, for they do not know what they do" (Luke 23:34). It was the same love that caused Stephen to pray for those who were stoning him, "Lord, do not charge them with this sin" (Acts 7:60). It is the love that changed Saul the persecutor into Paul the servant of Christ, who became "all things to all men, that [he] might by all means save some" (1 Corinthians 9:22).

For my part, when I contemplate the Bible's picture of the fully developed fruit of the Holy Spirit, I am both humbled and inspired. Humbled, because I still have so far to go. Inspired, because I have caught a glimpse of something more beautiful than anything that this world has to offer.

It is this picture that helps me, in Paul's words, keep "reaching forward to those things which are ahead." The days will not be easy; they rarely are in battle. But the goal, the prize, is "the upward call of God in Christ Jesus" (Philippians 3:13–14). Are you with me? Let's press on.

Part 3

Battle in the Heavenlies

15

∞∞∞

The Spirit of Antichrist

We are living in a time when the battle between the Kingdom of God and the kingdom of Satan is heating up as never before. I believe this is because we are nearing the return of Christ—and the ultimate destruction of Satan's kingdom.

In this part of the book we will explore several views of this progressing battle—angelic intervention, spiritual protection, weapons, to name just a few topics. I want to begin by examining one of the main outworkings of Satan's kingdom because it defines the core of our spiritual battle: Satan's opposition to God and to the Church of Jesus Christ. This opposition is manifested in something that I call the spirit of antichrist. This, as we will see, is distinct from the one person called the Antichrist, who, in turn, is distinct from the many antichrists that have arisen throughout history.

This spirit and these persons are described primarily in John's teaching:

Little children, it is the last hour; and as you have heard that the Antichrist is coming, even now many antichrists have come, by which we know that it is the last hour. They went out from us, but they were not of us; for if they had been of us, they would have continued with us; but they went out that they might be made manifest, that none of them were of us. But you have an anointing from the Holy One, and you know all things. I have not written to you because you do not know the truth, but because you know it, and that no lie is of the truth. Who is a liar but he who denies that Jesus is the Christ? He is antichrist who denies the Father and the Son. Whoever denies the Son does not have the Father either; he who acknowledges the Son has the Father also.

1 John 2:18–23

Let me explain the real meaning of the term *antichrist*. The word *Christ* is from a Greek word *christos*, which exactly corresponds to the Hebrew word *Mashiach* from which we get Messiah. So when we say "antichrist," that means anti-Messiah.

Anti is a Greek preposition. It has two meanings and both of them apply. First of all, it means "against." So the first operation is against Messiah. The second meaning is "in place of." The ultimate purpose is to put a false messiah in place of the true Messiah. So the total operation is in two phases. When you begin to recognize that, you will see that the spirit of antichrist is extremely active almost throughout the whole professing Church.

I have friends who belong to a church in the old-line evangelical stream. And they said to me, "In our church you can talk about Buddha, you can talk about Socrates, you can talk about Martin Luther King, and no one gets upset. But if you talk about Jesus everybody gets upset." That is the spirit of antichrist. But bear in mind that that is not the end of Satan's purpose. His purpose is to replace the true Messiah with a false messiah.

Further in John's teaching, we read:

By this you know the Spirit of God: Every spirit that confesses that Jesus [the Messiah] has come in the flesh is of God, and every spirit that does not confess that Jesus [the Messiah] has come in the flesh is not of God. And this is the spirit of the Antichrist, which you have heard was coming, and is now already in the world.

1 John 4:2–3

If we look at this passage along with the passage quoted earlier, we see the three forms of *antichrist*. First of all, there are many antichrists. In the course of human history, many antichrists have appeared and been manifested.

Secondly, there is *the Antichrist*—one specific person. That is the final manifestation, the final product of the spirit of antichrist, which has not yet been revealed in human history. I believe his shadow has already fallen across the stage, but we have not seen the actual person. But at the end of this age, Scripture makes it clear, there will be one final, supremely evil, supremely powerful ruler, who will dominate the human race for a brief period, who will be the Antichrist.

The third form is the *spirit of antichrist*. The spirit of antichrist is the spirit that operates through every antichrist. The closer we get to the end of the age, the more the spirit of antichrist is going to intensify and the more we will find ourselves engaging it in battle.

The Spirit of Antichrist

John has given us four identifying marks of the spirit of antichrist. These are very important. First of all, this spirit gets its start in association with God's people:

They went out from us, but they were not of us; for if they had been of us, they would have continued with us; but they went out that they might be made manifest, that none of them were of us.

1 John 2:19

So this spirit of antichrist always begins in some way in association with the people of God. But it does not really belong there, and in due course that will be made manifest.

The second mark of this spirit is that it denies that Jesus is the Messiah, as we see in 1 John 2:22: "Who is a liar but he who denies that Jesus is the [Messiah]?"

And then John continues with the third mark: "He is antichrist who denies the Father and the Son." Notice this: The spirit of antichrist does not deny the existence of God. In fact, the Antichrist will claim to be God's representative. What the spirit does deny is the relationship of the Father and the Son within the Godhead.

And the fourth mark of this spirit, given in 1 John 4, is that it denies the Messiah *has come*—it probably believes in the Messiah who *will come*, but denies that the Messiah has already come.

Now I want to look at a historical—yet somewhat controversial—example of the spirit of antichrist. I have certainly no desire to offend anybody or attack other religions. What I want to do is present the truth.

A main manifestation of the spirit of antichrist is Islam, the religion of Mohammed. In light of the events of September 11, 2001, in America, I believe it is important for Christians to be well informed about Islam.

Mohammed arose in the seventh century in the Arabian peninsula, claimed to be a prophet and claimed to receive from an archangel the revelation of the religion that became Islam. He also claimed that Islam was the true fulfillment of the Old and the New Testaments. He claimed that Christians and the gospels had perverted the real truth, but he was restoring it. That is the basic claim of Mohammed. He first believed that because he rejected idolatry and because he rejected the claims of Christianity, the Jewish people would follow him. When they did not follow him, he turned against them—and became a persecutor of them.

It is a tragedy that many Christians in the West have so misunderstood and underestimated Islam. In Moslem countries throughout the centuries, Christians and Jews have been given the title *dimmy,* which means second-class people. While it is true that Islam has not been guilty of anything so terrible as the Holocaust, it has a long record of thirteen centuries of suppression of and contempt for Christianity and Judaism.

Islam bears most of the marks of the spirit of antichrist. It started in association with the Old and New Testaments. It claimed to be the outworking of that revelation of God. But it denies certain basic fundamentals of the Christian faith, like the atoning death of Jesus on the cross. Mohammed taught that Jesus did not die, but that an angel came and spirited Him away before He died. Because there is no death, there is no atonement and because there is no atonement, there is no forgiveness. No Moslem has the assurance of sins forgiven at any time.

Second, Islam absolutely denies that Jesus is the Son of God. You can talk to the Moslems about Jesus as a prophet, and they will give you careful attention. In fact, the Koran acknowledges Jesus as a prophet—even as a Savior, even as a Messiah. But when you say He is the Son of God, you bring out the most intense, bitter opposition. In the famous mosque in Jerusalem that is called the Dome of the Rock—built on the site of what was the Temple of Solomon—the Arabic inscriptions around it say, twice: "God has no need of a son."

If you want to get a better picture of the beliefs and teachings of Islam, I recommend a book by my friend Jim Croft titled *The Muslim Masquerade.* Jim has researched this topic extensively, and in this book he supports his opinions with direct quotes from the Koran.

The Person Known as Antichrist

The final manifestation of the spirit of antichrist will be *the* Antichrist. I believe this is still in the future. I want to examine some passages of Scripture so that you are not unaware of what Satan is planning.

In 2 Thessalonians 2, Paul dealt with the appearance, revelation and manifestation of the Antichrist. He also addressed preparation for the Lord's return. These actions are closely intertwined, because the final satanic act before the return of the Lord will be the revealing of the Antichrist. Paul says, in fact, that the Lord will destroy the Antichrist with the brightness of His coming.

In 2 Thessalonians 2:1–2 we read:

> Now, brethren, concerning the coming of our Lord Jesus Christ and our gathering together to Him, we ask you, not to be soon shaken in mind or troubled, either by spirit or by word or by letter, as if from us.

The word *coming* here is the word *parousia* in Greek, which is normally used for the Second Coming of Jesus.

Paul wrote, "[Don't be] shaken . . . or troubled, either by spirit or by word or by letter, as if from us," because he knew that many Christians would be prepared to believe specific predictions as to when Jesus would return. I certainly have heard plenty of these predictions over the course of my ministry, and I am amazed at the multitudes of Christians that become fixated on them.

Paul continued:

> [Don't be deceived] as though the day of Christ had come. Let no one deceive you by any means; for that Day will not come unless the falling away comes first, and the man of sin is revealed, the son of perdition.
>
> 2 Thessalonians 2:2–3

The term "falling away" in Greek is *apostacia*, meaning an apostasy—a deliberate rejection of revealed truth.

This verse offers two titles of the Antichrist. First, he is the "man of sin"—or man of lawlessness. He is the supreme embodiment of man's rebellion against God and rejection of God's laws. He is also called the "son of perdition," the one who is headed for a lost eternity. Judas Iscariot is the only other person in the New Testament who is called son of perdition. He was a false apostle.

So we see three different names for the same being: the Antichrist, the man of lawlessness, the son of perdition. And we are given one other important name in Revelation 13. This is part of the vision that John had:

> I saw a beast rising up out of the sea, having seven heads and ten horns, and on his horns ten crowns, and on his heads a blasphemous name. Now the beast which I saw was like a leopard, his feet were like the feet of a bear, and his mouth like the mouth of a lion. The dragon gave him his power, his throne, and great authority. And I saw one of his heads as if it had been mortally wounded, and his deadly wound was healed. And all the world marveled and followed the beast. So they worshiped the dragon who gave authority to the beast; and they worshiped the beast, saying, "Who is like the beast? Who is able to make war with him?"
>
> Revelation 13:1–4

Here we see the fourth title: "the beast"—a person who is going to arise to whom Satan (the dragon) will give his power. Why will Satan give his power to this person? Because that will enable this person to gain dominion over the entire human race and to persuade the entire human race to do the one thing that Satan wants most: to worship him. This is his goal. He has been working on this patiently for many centuries, and he is very near to its achievement.

Notice one of his heads had been "mortally wounded" and healed. There is a sort of false resurrection here. I do not know if this person will be assassinated, but he will apparently be dead, and he will return to life.

In his vision, John saw a scroll in the hand of God, and there was no one who was found worthy to open it. So John was weeping.

> But one of the elders said to me, "Do not weep. Behold, the Lion of the tribe of Judah, the Root of David, has prevailed to open the scroll and to loose its seven seals." And I looked, and behold, in the midst of the throne and of the four living creatures, and in the midst of the elders, stood a Lamb as though it had been slain.
>
> Revelation 5:5–6

John was looking for a Lion, but the Lion is a Lamb. That is a deliberate contradiction. God's appointed ruler does not have the nature of the beast. He has the nature of the Lamb. And He is highly exalted above all others because He laid down His life. He humbled Himself. He went the way of meekness and humility, because He did not resist His arresters and His persecutors. I believe that the Church in these days is going to need to display the same nature. And I don't believe it is easy.

We have seen that the people worshiped the beast. And they all were convinced it was hopeless to make war with the beast. I am not certain what sort of circumstances will convince "all the world" that it is futile to fight back. When you consider the age of technology and weaponry in which we currently live, it is easy to believe that the situation pictured here could be close upon us.

In Revelation 13:6–7 we see the Antichrist take action:

> Then he opened his mouth in blasphemy against God, to blaspheme His name, His tabernacle, and those who dwell in heaven. It was granted to him to make war with the saints and to overcome them.

He is the open challenger of God. He is not a secret enemy; he shakes his fist in the face of Almighty God. And who do you think granted him permission to make war with—and overcome—the saints? I presume it is God, which is a very sobering thought. Let's never forget that Christianity is not all easy victory.

Let's go further and look at verse 8: "All who dwell on the earth will worship him, whose names have not been written in the Book of Life of the Lamb slain from the foundation of the world." What a dramatic statement! The entire human race will worship him—except those God has chosen for Himself.

As That Day Approaches

Our battle plan, then, becomes clear. Look again at 2 Thessalonians 2:3: "Let no one deceive you by any means; for that Day [the coming of the Lord] will not come unless the falling away comes first, and the man of sin is revealed."

I believe this falling away is taking place in the world today. Through the centuries there have been church leaders who were wicked, but they did not openly deny the great basic truths of the Christian faith. In fact, those truths were the means they used to support their power. But the twentieth century saw church leaders deny the great basic truths of the Christian faith: the deity of Jesus, His virgin birth, His atoning death, His physical resurrection and His return. I do not believe this existed in any previous century. I believe that we are already confronted with the apostasy. Always remember that the Church is the bulwark against error. Satan has to penetrate the Church before he can complete his plans.

And he is not working alone. Fallen angels have interacted with humans throughout our history. In the next chapter, we will discover a less-well-known aspect of their intervention—and how we should respond.

16

Angelic Intervention in Human Lives

In giving instructions about the conduct of worship in the New Testament Church, Paul writes that a certain course of action should be taken "because of the angels" (1 Corinthians 11:10). Paul takes it for granted that when Christians meet for worship, angels will also be present and will participate.

More than once when Ruth and I were worshiping together, she heard the angels singing. We realized that we were privileged to experience a tiny part of the total worship of the universe, spanning both heaven and earth. I have heard similar testimony from other Christians.

The writer of Hebrews says that God's angels are "all ministering spirits sent forth to minister for those who will inherit salvation" (Hebrews 1:14). The Greek phrase translated "ministering spirits" describes specifically spirits who perform priestly acts of worship. In the New Testament Church, heaven and earth were blended together in worship.

Successive Angelic Rebellions

The Bible reveals a succession of angelic rebellions against God. The first—and the most significant—was the original rebellion of Lucifer (an archangel) described in Isaiah:

> "How you are fallen from heaven, O Lucifer, son of the morning! How you are cut down to the ground, you who weakened the nations! For you have said in your heart: 'I will ascend into heaven, I will exalt my throne above the stars of God; I will also sit on the mount of the congregation on the farthest sides of the north; I will ascend above the heights of the clouds, I will be like [equal to] the Most High.'"
>
> Isaiah 14:12–14

For my part, I believe that the divine Person whose position Satan aspired to was not God the Father but God the Son (revealed later in human history as Jesus of Nazareth). The conflict between these two came to its climax at the cross, where Satan apparently defeated Jesus, but, in actual fact, Jesus stripped Satan of all his weapons and left him totally defeated. "Having disarmed principalities and powers [of Satan], He [Jesus] made a public spectacle of them, triumphing over them in it [the cross]" (Colossians 2:15).

In Revelation 12:3–4 Satan is depicted as "a great, fiery red dragon" whose "tail drew a third of the stars of heaven." Apparently as an archangel, Lucifer (now Satan) had authority over one-third of heaven's angels, who followed him in his rebellion and were, with him, cast out of heaven. Satan and the angels who followed him then established a rival kingdom (see Ephesians 6:12).

Although Satan's destiny has been irrevocably settled by his defeat at the cross, final judgment on him will not be carried out until the close of the Millenium. At that time Satan—together with the Antichrist—will be "cast into the lake of fire and brimstone. . . . And they will be tormented day and night forever and ever" (Revelation 20:10).

Fallen Angels before the Flood

A further transgression on the part of angels is described in Genesis 6:1–2:

> Now it came to pass, when men began to multiply on the face of the earth, and daughters were born to them, that the sons of God saw the daughters of men, that they were beautiful; and they took wives for themselves of all whom they chose.

Who are these "sons of God"? They are twice referred to in the book of Job. First, "There was a day when the sons of God came to present themselves before the LORD, and Satan also came among them" (Job 1:6). And again when God asks Job: "Where were you . . . when the morning stars sang together, and all the sons of God shouted for joy?" (Job 38:4, 7). Obviously, in both these passages these "sons of God" are angelic beings. No human beings were present when God laid the foundation of the earth.

There are two passages in the New Testament that describe God's judgment on the angels who sinned in this way with human women. Jude 6 says:

> And the angels who did not keep their positions of authority but abandoned their own home [heaven]—these he has kept in darkness, bound with everlasting chains for judgment on the great Day.

NIV

These are not the angels who participated in Satan's original rebellion, because Satan and his angels are not yet confined, but are free and active in "the heavenly places." The sin of the angels that Jude refers to was that they abandoned their appointed dwelling place in heaven and came down to the plane of earth, where they cohabited with human women.

Jude then continues:

> In a similar way, Sodom and Gomorrah and the surrounding towns gave themselves up to sexual immorality and perversion. They serve as an example of those who suffer the punishment of eternal fire.
>
> verse 7, NIV

Jude compares the fallen angels of Noah's day with the people of Sodom and Gomorrah because both groups were guilty of the same sin of sexual immorality and perversion.

Peter likewise joins together the fallen angels of Noah's day with the people of Sodom and Gomorrah:

> For if God did not spare the angels who sinned, but cast them down to hell and delivered them into chains of darkness, to be reserved for judgment; and did not spare the ancient world, but saved Noah, one of eight people, a preacher of righteousness, bringing in the flood on the world of the ungodly; and turning the cities of Sodom and Gomorrah into ashes, condemned them to destruction, making them an example to those who afterward would live ungodly; and delivered righteous Lot. . . .
>
> 2 Peter 2:4–7

In both cases their sin was unnatural sex. In verse 4, where the English translation says "cast them down to *hell*," the Greek word used is actually *tartarus*, a word that occurs frequently in Greek literature. *Tartarus* has been defined as "a place of confinement as far below Hades as Hades is below earth."

It is amazing how long the Lord will tolerate some forms of sin in the world, but there are certain boundaries that God watches over jealously. One such boundary is that which prohibits sexual perversion, whether it is between angels and human beings or between human beings of the same sex. When that boundary is crossed, God's severest judgments will follow quickly. In one case, judgment came in the form of the flood; in the other it instantaneously wiped out the population of two entire cities.

Similar Sins in Our Day

The Bible indicates that intercourse between angels and human women did not permanently cease at the time of the flood.

> The Nephilim were on the earth in those days—and also afterward—when the sons of God went to the daughters of men and had children by them. They were the heroes of old, men of renown.
>
> Genesis 6:4, NIV

The Hebrew word *nephilim* is directly derived from the Hebrew verb *naphal*, which means "to fall." *Nephilim*, therefore, are "fallen ones"—that is, fallen angels. There were *nephilim* on the earth "in those days" (that is, at the time of the flood)—and also "afterward" (that is, after the flood).

Those who were born in this later period out of this unnatural union were called *heroes*. Greek mythology abounds with descriptions of such heroes. They were born when beings whom the Greeks called *gods* had intercourse with human women. These gods were supernaturally powerful beings who came down from a higher plane of existence. The Bible calls them *nephilim*. They were, in fact, fallen angels.

138

To give but a few examples, Zeus (the "father" of the gods) was said to have taken the form of a swan and united with a woman called Leda, who bore him three children. On another occasion, in the form of a bull, Zeus had intercourse with Europa, who also bore him three sons. Another god—Poseidon, the god of the ocean—united with a human woman and she bore him a son called Theseus, who became one of the most famous of the Greek heroes.

Many other examples could be added. These myths are like a cracked mirror, giving a distorted representation of events that are accurately summed up in Genesis 6:4.

As in the Days of Noah

In Luke 17:26, Jesus warns us: "And as it was in the days of Noah, so it will be also in the days of the Son of Man." In other words, conditions that marked the days of Noah will again characterize the period just before the present age closes.

In Noah's day "the earth also was corrupt before God, and the earth was filled with violence" (Genesis 6:11). Both of these features are being manifestly reproduced before our eyes today: moral corruption and continually escalating violence.

In Noah's day, too, humanity was invaded by angels from a higher plane who made human women the objects of their lust. It is interesting to note that for more than half a century, the media have reported "eyewitness accounts" of "visitors from outer space." Might some of these be demonic appearances? Even if we write off most of these accounts as fabrications, that does not alter the fact that Scripture says the conditions from the days of Noah will be reproduced. I believe that fallen angels are again at work on planet earth.

If the above interpretation of Scripture is correct, it imparts a fresh urgency to Paul's warnings given in 1 Corinthians

11:2–16, in which he discusses the headship of Christ over men, and men over women. Paul did not view the Church as a little group of people tucked away on their own in some religious building. Rather he viewed the Church as part of a vast, action-packed drama spanning both earth and heaven. Participation in their meetings was not limited to human beings but could also include angels, both good and evil.

In particular, Paul warned that human women participating in the worship of the Church needed to be aware of the possible presence of both good and evil angels. Their appropriate response was to have a suitable covering on their heads. This is the verse I referred to at the opening of this chapter: "For this reason the woman ought to have a symbol of authority on her head, because of the angels" (1 Corinthians 11:10). In this way, they affirmed that they were under the authority that Christ has vested in His Church. They also paid due respect to the good angels who might be present and at the same time protected themselves against impure spiritual influences that might proceed from evil angels.

The instructions concerning worship that Paul gives in 1 Corinthians 11:2–16 can be summed up in one word: *reverence.*

"Where Is My Reverence?"

In the time of Malachi, the Lord charged His people with insincerity in their worship. They were very religious, yet they were irreverent. In Malachi 1:6 the Lord says: "A son honors his father, and a servant his master. If then I am the Father, where is My honor? And if I am a Master, where is My reverence?" Then in Malachi 1:14 He concludes: "For I am a great King . . . and My name is to be feared among the nations."

Almost all cultures have certain rules of conduct that govern the way people relate to their king. We call these rules *protocol*.

Like an earthly king, the Lord, too, has His *protocol*. Some of the requirements of heaven's protocol are stated in 1 Corinthians 11:2–16. They remind us that Christians in their worship are not just a little isolated group on their own. On the contrary, Paul says, "We have been made a spectacle to the world [the universe], both to angels and to men" (1 Corinthians 4:9). Since this reference to "angels" includes both good and evil angels, we need to study and follow the requirements of heaven's protocol. This is not only important as a token of our respect for the Lord, but also in our own best interests.

17

Warfare in Heavenly Places

In the previous chapter, I pointed out that Christians in their worship must reckon with the presence of angels—both good and evil. In particular, Scripture reveals the activity on earth of fallen angels before and also after the flood in Noah's day.

I referred, too, to the original rebellion of Lucifer—now known as Satan—described in Isaiah 14:12–15. In this chapter I will examine that rebellion and its consequences. Important insights into Lucifer's rebellion are provided in Ezekiel 28:1–19, which depicts two persons—the *prince* of Tyre and the *king* of Tyre.

Satan's Motives and Means

The prince of Tyre apparently claimed to be a god, but in Ezekiel he is depicted as a man dying at the hand of invaders: "Will you still say before him who slays you, 'I am a god'? But you shall be a man, and not a god, in the hand of him who slays you" (Ezekiel 28:9).

The king of Tyre, on the other hand, is an angelic being who originally occupied a place of great honor in heaven:

"You were in Eden, the garden of God; every precious stone was your covering. . . . You were the anointed cherub who covers [the throne of God with your wings]; I established you; you were on the holy mountain of God; you walked back and forth in the midst of fiery stones. You were perfect in your ways from the day you were created, till iniquity was found in you."

verses 13–15

Lucifer was a resplendent figure, but he was a created being who rebelled against his Creator.

Continuing with verse 16: "By the abundance of your *trading* you became filled with violence within, and you sinned" (emphasis added). In Leviticus 19:16, a word from the same root as that translated *trading* describes "a talebearer" who goes about among his people. This suggests that Lucifer went about among the angels under him, undermining their loyalty to God and persuading them to join him in his rebellion. Perhaps he may have made suggestions, such as: "God doesn't really appreciate you. If I were in the place of God, I would give you a much higher position."

God—to whose eyes all things are naked and open (see Hebrews 4:13)—was undoubtedly aware of Lucifer's activity, but gave him time to perfect his scheme of rebellion before taking action against him. "Your heart was lifted up because of your beauty; you corrupted your wisdom for the sake of your splendor" (Ezekiel 28:17). Lucifer's outstanding wisdom and beauty filled his heart with pride and thus became the cause of his downfall.

This also was the motive attributed to Lucifer in Isaiah 14:13–14: "For you have said in your heart: 'I will ascend into heaven, I will exalt my throne above the stars of God. . . . I will ascend above the heights of the clouds, I will be like [equal to] the Most High.'"

We all need to bear in mind continually that *pride* was the cause of Lucifer's downfall. It is also the main motive that Satan uses in tempting human beings to sin. Pride has caused the downfall of more men and women than all the other sins put together.

The relationship between the prince of Tyre (a man) and the king of Tyre (a heavenly being) exemplifies the way in which throughout history satanic angels in the heavenly places have intervened in affairs on earth by controlling earthly rulers.

Their relationship is also a preview of the relationship that will develop between Satan and the Antichrist. As we saw in the last chapter, Satan will use the Antichrist to gain for himself the worship of the whole world. "So they [the whole world] worshiped the dragon [Satan] . . . and they worshiped the beast [the Antichrist]" (Revelation 13:4).

Since worship is due always and only to God, by gaining the worship of the whole world for himself Satan will be making one last claim to what he originally aspired to: equality with God.

The Location of Satan's Kingdom

Satan and the angels who joined him in his rebellion against God were cast out of heaven, but they have not yet been cast down to earth. Paul describes them as "spiritual hosts of wickedness in the heavenly places" (Ephesians 6:12).

In Colossians 1:16, Paul lists the four main orders of heavenly beings who were created by God through Christ:

144

thrones, dominions, principalities (rulerships) and powers (authorities). In Ephesians 6:12, the two highest orders that Paul mentions as having joined in Satan's rebellion are rulerships and authorities. This indicates that neither thrones nor dominions were enticed by Satan into joining in his rebellion.

From its opening verse, the Bible indicates that the earth is singular, but the heavens are plural: "God created the heavens [plural] and the earth [singular]" (Genesis 1:1). Paul speaks of a man "caught up to the third heaven" (2 Corinthians 12:2). Obviously, there cannot be a third heaven unless there is also a first and a second.

Paul says that in the third heaven this man was "caught up into Paradise and heard inexpressible words, which it is not lawful [or possible] for a man to utter" (2 Corinthians 12:4). This indicates that the third—and highest—heaven is a place of the utmost holiness, the actual dwelling place of God Himself. If the first heaven is the one visible from earth, then there must be a "second" intermediate heaven somewhere between the visible heaven and the third heaven, which is God's dwelling place. I believe that this intermediate heaven is the location of Satan's kingdom.

The confirmation of this idea comes from the book of Daniel. In Daniel 10:2–12, after Daniel had given himself to three weeks of mourning and partial fasting, a heavenly being appeared to him and spoke to him:

> "Do not fear, Daniel, for from the first day that you set your heart to understand, and to humble yourself before your God, your words were heard; and I have come because of your words."
>
> Daniel 10:12

The heavenly being then refers to three other angelic beings: to Michael, an archangel of God, and to the prince of

145

Persia and the prince of Greece. These latter two are angels—
or perhaps archangels—of Satan (see Daniel 10:13–21).

In order to reach Daniel on earth, the angel sent from
God had to meet and overcome satanic angels who opposed
him. This confirms that Satan's kingdom is located in "the
heavenly places"—somewhere between the heaven that is
God's dwelling place and the heaven that is visible from
earth. It also reveals several important facts about prayer
and spiritual warfare:

1. The initiative in these events came from Daniel on
   earth. It was his prayer and fasting that set in motion the activity of God's angels in the heavenly
   places.
2. The angels in the satanic kingdom opposed the angel
   sent to Daniel from the third heaven (the heaven
   where God dwells).
3. These satanic angels were so powerful that it took God's
   angels three weeks to break through their opposition.
4. Daniel's prayers played a vital part in the ultimate
   victory.

Lessons We Can Learn

This account of Daniel's praying contains important lessons that can make our prayers more effective in battle.

1. Our praying can set in motion the forces of God in
   heaven. God sometimes waits for us on earth to take
   the initiative.
2. To reach the throne of God in heaven, our prayers
   must pass through a satanic kingdom in the heavenly
   places. For this they must be supernaturally empow-
   ered: "For the kingdom of God is not in word but in
   power" (1 Corinthians 4:20).

146

3. Our prayers, therefore, need to be enforced by praise and thanksgiving. This serves as a "booster rocket" to carry them up to the throne of God. Supplications, prayers and intercessions must be accompanied by giving of thanks (see 1 Timothy 2:1).
4. Fasting increases our spiritual sensitivity and adds supernatural power to praying. Some satanic forces will yield only to prayer that is accompanied by fasting.

In the next chapter, I will deal with various forms of spiritual protection that God has provided for us in our conflict with Satan's kingdom of rebellious angels.

18

Principles of Spiritual Protection

When we are born again as Christians into the Kingdom of God, we discover that we are caught up in a war with an opposing spiritual kingdom—the kingdom of Satan. In this we have no option. Because the kingdom to which we belong is at war, we are part of the war. We discover, too, that we have various kinds of enemies, but the most powerful and the most formidable is a kingdom of rebellious angels in the heavenly places, under the rule of God's archenemy, Satan.

Because we have such powerful enemies, we all need to avail ourselves of the protection that God has provided. In this chapter we will review three uncompromising demands of God that apply to all Christians.

Understanding Authority

As we have noted, Paul said that Christian women need the protection of scriptural authority over them—symbolized by appropriate coverings on their heads. But this is only one example of a principle that applies more generally to all Christians—both male and female. Every Christian needs the protection of being under appropriate scriptural authority.

Luke 7:1–10 records how a Roman centurion sent some Jewish elders to Jesus to ask for the healing of his servant, who was at death's door. Jesus offered to go and pray for the healing of the servant, but the centurion responded:

> "Lord, do not trouble Yourself, for I am not worthy that You should enter under my roof. Therefore I did not even think myself worthy to come to You. But say the word, and my servant will be healed. For I also am a man placed under authority, having soldiers under me. And I say to one, 'Go,' and he goes; and to another, 'Come,' and he comes; and to my servant, 'Do this,' and he does it."
>
> Luke 7:6–8

By saying, "I *also* am a man placed under authority," the centurion recognized that the authority of Jesus in the spiritual realm was analogous to the authority that he had in the military realm as a centurion in the Roman army. In each case, their authority was derived from submission to a higher source. For the centurion, the source was the Roman Emperor. For Jesus, the source was God the Father.

Note, too, that the centurion did not say—as many would have done—"I *have* authority," but "I am *under* authority." He affirmed a basic principle of Scripture: to *have* authority one must be *under* authority. Authority always flows *downward*.

After His resurrection, Jesus said, "All authority has been given to Me in heaven and on earth" (Matthew 28:18). There are chains of authority that descend from God the Father through Jesus the Son into every situation in the universe. Paul explains that there is a descending chain of authority that is designed to work in every family on earth: "The head of every man is Christ, the head of woman is man, and the head of Christ is God" (1 Corinthians 11:3). In the case of a married couple, for instance, authority descends from God the Father through Jesus the Son to the husband and through the husband to the wife.

But what is true in the home applies to every other department of life. It applies to all Christians. Every Christian needs the protection of being under an appropriate authority. *A Christian not under authority is an unprotected Christian.*

Authority in the Church

The first demand of God that helps ensure our protection is respect for Christ's authority operating in and through each local church. Paul says that God gave Jesus to be "head over all things to the church" (Ephesians 1:22). The Greek word for church is *ekklesia*. In its original meaning, *ekklesia* denoted a group of citizens in a city-state (such as Athens) who were the collective government of the city. When applied to Christians, it indicates that in His redemptive acts Jesus exercises His authority through the Church, which is His *ekklesia*.

To be under Christ's authority, therefore, means to be rightly related to His Church. We cannot claim the protection of Christ's authority over us if we do not respect the authority that He has vested in His Church.

This is illustrated in the appointment of Paul as an apostle. Paul calls himself "an apostle of Jesus Christ, by the commandment of God our Savior and the Lord Jesus Christ, our hope" (1 Timothy 1:1). The ultimate authority of Paul's apostleship was a decision made in heaven by God the Father and God the Son. But by definition an "apostle" is "one sent forth." Paul's apostleship did not become effective, therefore, until he was "sent forth" from a local church in Antioch.

In Acts 13:1 Paul (still called Saul) is listed as one of five men described as "prophets and teachers." Then, in response to a direction from the Holy Spirit, the other three men laid hands on Barnabas and Saul and sent them forth. After that, both men are called *apostles* (see Acts 14:4, 14). The apostleship of Paul was determined in heaven, but it only became effective when it was acknowledged and acted upon by a local church on earth.

In more than fifty years of worldwide ministry, I have always sought to recognize and respect the authority of Christ operating through a local church. First Lydia (my first wife) and I—and then Ruth (my second wife) and I—always identified with a local congregation wherever our place of residence was. When we went out on our ministry journeys, we were officially sent out from a local church. When we returned, we gave a report to the church that sent us out. This was the practice established by Paul and Barnabas in Acts 13:3 and 14:26–27.

Some Christians are looking for a perfect church. I have to acknowledge that I have never yet found such a church. But then I have to acknowledge also that if I ever should find such a church, I could not join it, because after I joined it would no longer be perfect! Meanwhile, I am grateful for everything good I have received through various "imperfect" local churches.

Paul also gives a second picture of God's people here on earth. He says "the church, which is His [Christ's] *body*" (Ephesians 1:22–23, emphasis added). Paul develops this theme in 1 Corinthians 12:27: "Now you are the body of Christ, and members individually." He uses various examples from the physical body to emphasize that, as

151

Christians, we are all interdependent and we all need each other.

The most complete and authoritative picture of the Church as the Body of Christ is given in Ephesians. It is most significant, therefore, that throughout this epistle Paul speaks consistently of Christians in the plural. He has virtually nothing to say to or about individual Christians. In Ephesians 1:3–12, for example, Paul says the following: God has blessed *us*—He chose *us*—He predestined *us*—He made *us* accepted—*we* have redemption—He has made known to *us* the mystery of His will—*we* have obtained an inheritance—*we* should be to the praise of His glory.

A careful reading of the rest of the epistle will confirm that this is its message from beginning to end. There are no promises and no prayers for any individual. Only in the last six verses is there one brief exception: Paul closes by asking for special prayer for himself.

This focus on the collective body of Christ comes to its climax in Ephesians 6:10–18, where Paul speaks about our spiritual warfare. In verse 12, all the key words are in the plural—both those that refer to God's people and those that refer to the opposing forces: *We* wrestle against *principalities—powers—rulers—hosts.*

The spiritual warfare thus depicted is not a conflict between individuals, but a vast war between opposing armies. There is no room here for "lone rangers" pursuing their individual goals. Victory will require controlled and concerted action by God's people working together as members of one body. This will demand discipline and a readiness to submit to scriptural authority.

Understanding Lawlessness

One feature of the close of the present age concerning which Jesus warned His disciples was an upsurge of *law-*

lessness: "And because lawlessness will abound, the love of many will grow cold" (Matthew 24:12). Jesus indicated that many Christians would be infected by this prevailing lawlessness and as a result their love for God and His people would grow cold.

The essence of lawlessness is a rejection of authority. This has become an obvious feature of our contemporary culture. There is a widespread contempt for any rules or regulations that interfere with each person's individual liberty. People are forceful in asserting their "rights," yet very reluctant to acknowledge their corresponding responsibilities. At times, the consequence is a condition bordering on anarchy. As Christians, we have to guard ourselves against this kind of attitude. We are required to show our respect for legitimate secular authority.

But first and foremost, we must cultivate and maintain an attitude of respect and obedience toward God our Father and toward Jesus our Savior. This will be expressed in a corresponding attitude of respect and obedience toward God's Word, the Scripture.

Jesus said: "If anyone loves Me, he will keep My word. . . . He who does not love Me does not keep My words" (John 14:23–24). We may make claims to love God and we may even pray long and eloquent prayers or preach long and eloquent sermons, but as the last resort we really do not honor and obey God more than we honor and obey His Word. In the midst of prevailing lawlessness it would be appropriate for each of us to make a fresh affirmation of our unreserved and total submission to the authority of Scripture. "All Scripture is given by inspiration of God" (2 Timothy 3:16).

Lawlessness in Our Personal Relationships

The second and third demands of God that help ensure our protection involve our personal relationships:

They are forgiveness and submission. These are two main areas in which our submission to God and His Word will be tested, and Jesus has laid down some very strict rules.

Concerning forgiving other people, for instance, He said:

> "And whenever you stand praying, if you have anything against anyone, forgive him, that your Father in heaven may also forgive you your trespasses. But if you do not forgive, neither will your Father in heaven forgive your trespasses."
>
> Mark 11:25–26

Again, at the end of the pattern prayer which Jesus taught His disciples in Matthew 6:9–13, He added only one comment: "For if you forgive men their trespasses, your heavenly Father will also forgive you. But if you do not forgive men their trespasses, neither will your Father forgive your trespasses" (Matthew 6:14–15).

We always need to remember that forgiving another person is not an expression of emotion but an act of *self-discipline*. For this we can depend upon the Holy Spirit, who is a Spirit "of power, of love and of self-discipline" (2 Timothy 1:7, NIV).

Self-discipline is also required to produce the kind of attitude Paul describes in Ephesians 5:21: "submitting to one another in the fear of God." This attitude of mutual submission is the key to right relationships both in the home and in the Church.

Christians who refuse to forgive others or to submit to one another are in defiance of Scripture. Their root problem is *lawlessness*. They have opened themselves up to the spirit prevailing in the world around them. It will inevitably make them vulnerable to the evil angels who are their relentless enemies in the heavenly places.

Obedience and Covering

We are confronted, then, with three areas in which Scripture reveals clear, uncompromising demands of God that apply to all Christians. The first is respect for Christ's authority operating in and through each local church. The second is unqualified forgiveness for all who have wronged us or harmed us. The third is an attitude of submissiveness toward all our fellow Christians.

Obedience in these three areas provides Christians with a covering of scriptural authority that protects them from the attacks of satanic angels in the heavenly places. Disobedience, conversely, inevitably makes Christians vulnerable to such attacks.

This chapter is written out of deep personal concern. On the basis of many years of experience in the Body of Christ, I am convinced that the consequences of disobeying these three requirements of Scripture can be tragic in the extreme. I believe that it is one main reason why many fine, dedicated servants of the Lord have become casualties. I pray that God may grant us all a new respect for the authority of Christ vested in His Church and that He may renew in each of us an attitude of forgiveness and submissiveness.

19

The Weapons of
Our Warfare

We have learned thus far that when we become Christians, we are automatically involved in a vast spiritual war that spans both heaven and earth. Furthermore, our most powerful and dangerous enemies are a kingdom of evil angels whose headquarters are in the heavenlies.

In His wisdom and mercy God has provided us with all the weapons that we need to achieve victory. Because our warfare is in the spiritual realm, our weapons are also spiritual. Paul says that "the weapons of our warfare are not carnal [but by implication, spiritual] but mighty in God for pulling down strongholds" (2 Corinthians 10:4).

The strongholds that we attack are also spiritual. Over the centuries Satan has built them up in the hearts and minds of humanity. They are strongholds of fear, covetousness, hatred, idolatry, racial prejudice, religious superstition and many others.

It is these strongholds, by the way, that frustrate all attempts by politicians to negotiate real peace. The logical and political arguments in favor of negotiated settlements are not strong enough to break down the spiritual strongholds that stand in the way of peace.

True peace will only come to earth when the Kingdom of Christ is established here. This is the objective of our warfare as Christians and the purpose for which we use our spiritual weapons. It is to break down the spiritual strongholds in the hearts of men and women and to prepare the way for Christ to set up His Kingdom—first in their hearts and finally in the whole earth.

Paul lists in Ephesians 6:13–18 seven spiritual weapons—or items of spiritual equipment—that we need. He takes his examples from the equipment of a Roman legionary in his day. Here is the list.

1. The Girdle of Truth

In Paul's day both men and women normally wore long, loose garments that came down at least to their knees. Before undertaking any strenuous activity, the first thing they had to do was to gather up their loose garments and tuck them into their girdles. Only after this were they free to undertake any vigorous action. Hence the phrase that occurs several times in Scripture: "Gird up your loins."

Using the girdle of truth requires that we renounce every form of dishonesty or compromise. If we do not "tuck them up" out of our way, they will hamper our spiritual progress. We must be faithful to the truth of Scripture even when it is controversial or unpopular.

We must also be completely open and sincere in all our personal relationships. This is an essential condition of proper spiritual growth. Writing to new Christians, Peter says: "Therefore, laying aside all malice, all deceit, hypocrisy, envy, and all evil speaking, as newborn babes, desire the pure milk of the word, *that you may grow thereby*" (1 Peter 2:1–2, emphasis added).

Above all, we must be absolutely open and honest in our dealings with God Himself. This is a condition for receiving spiritual revelation. David says: "Behold, You desire truth in the inward parts, and in the hidden part You will make me to know wisdom" (Psalm 51:6).

God reveals His hidden wisdom only to those who have truth in their inward parts.

2. The Breastplate of Righteousness

The breastplate protects our *hearts*. In Proverbs 4:23 we are warned: "Keep [guard] your heart with all diligence, for out of it spring the issues of life." Our success in the spiritual life depends on maintaining a right heart relationship with both God and man. We must follow the example of Paul and "always strive to have a conscience without offense toward God and men" (Acts 24:16).

The kind of righteousness God looks for is not mere intellectual assent to doctrine. It is a condition of the heart, not the mind. "For with the *heart* one believes unto righteousness" (Romans 10:10, emphasis added).

Neither is it the observance of religious rules. Paul had been occupied with those for many years, but when he met Christ, his ambition changed—

> that I may gain Christ and be found in Him, not having my own righteousness, which is from the law, but that which is through faith in Christ, the righteousness which is from God by faith.
>
> Philippians 3:8–9

3. The Shoes of Preparation and Peace

Roman legionaries were equipped with strong sandals. These made them highly mobile. They could make long, forced marches at short notice.

As Christians, we need to be *mobile*—available to God for His purposes wherever and whenever He calls upon us—even at short notice or in unexpected circumstances. This requires *preparation*. We must familiarize ourselves with the basic truths of the Gospel and how to present them to an unbeliever.

Also, it is a gospel of *peace*. We can only communicate the Gospel effectively if we have real peace in our hearts—a peace that is not dependent on our external circumstances. To a troubled, perplexed sinner the tone of our voices may communicate our messages more effectively than the actual words that we speak.

4. The Shield of Faith

The word here translated *shield* is connected with the word for *door*. Its length was greater than its width. A trained soldier could so crouch down and draw his body in that he was completely protected. But he had to be fit and athletic. An overweight man would not be fully protected.

Our shield of faith must likewise be complete in all its dimensions. It must cover our total personality—spirit, soul and body. We must also be so spiritually trained and fit that we can draw ourselves together within an area that is completely covered by the promises of Scripture. Anything in our lives that is superfluous or self-indulgent will be outside the protection of our shield.

At times the arrows Satan uses against us are "fiery." They are designed not merely to wound but also to set on fire whatever they are aimed at. They can start fires of gossip or slander or division in families or even in whole congregations. But the shield of faith—vigilantly and effectively used—will not merely stop the arrows, it will *quench* them. It will extinguish the flames.

5. The Helmet of Salvation

Just as the breastplate protects our *hearts*, so the helmet protects our *minds*—our thought lives. The mind is the area in which Christians are most regularly attacked. Inside our minds there is often a continuing war. Satan seeks to insinuate thoughts that will disturb us or distract us or in some other way make us ineffective in our war against him.

God has taught me personally many lessons in this area. When I was first born again, I was continually assailed in my mind by depression or discouragement. I saw that I needed some effective protection in that area. When I read Paul's list of armor in Ephesians 6:13–18, I realized that it was the *helmet of salvation* that I needed. But then I said to myself, *I know that I am saved. Does that mean that I already have the helmet of salvation or is it something that I need to get after salvation?*

As I pondered this, I saw that the Christians in Ephesus to whom Paul was writing were already saved. Yet Paul still instructed them to *take* the helmet of salvation. Clearly, therefore, I needed to do the same. But what was this "helmet of salvation" that should be the protection for my mind?

Fortunately, I was using a Bible with cross-references in the margin. The cross-reference to Ephesians 6:17 was 1 Thessalonians 5:8: "and as a helmet the *hope* of salvation" (emphasis added). That Scripture revolutionized my thought life. If *pessimism* was my problem, then *optimism* was the logical solution.

I set myself to seek out—and in many cases to memorize—passages of Scripture that provided me with a basis for strong, continuing optimism. Today my mind is effectively protected!

Up to this point all the items of equipment that we have considered have been solely—or primarily—for purposes of *protection* or *defense*. Only at this point does Paul turn to weapons of *attack*. For this there is a logical and practical reason: If we attempt to attack before we have secured our defense, we are unprepared for the enemy's counterattack and we are likely to become casualties. This is one main reason why some Christians are wounded and become casualties.

We will turn now to the two remaining weapons.

6. The Sword of the Spirit

This sword, which, Paul says, is the Word of God, can be used for both attack and defense, but it is primarily a weapon of attack. Someone has said, "The best defense is a good attack"—and this is often true in the spiritual realm.

The word here translated as "word" is *rhema*, which usually denotes a word that is *spoken*. As we noted in chapter 12 on the indispensable Word, it is not having the Bible in our bookshelves or even on our nightstands that is effective. But when we take Scripture in our mouths and proclaim it boldly through our lips, then it becomes a sharp, two-edged sword.

Note, too, that it is "the sword of the [Holy] Spirit." We can take God's Word in our mouths, but it only achieves its full effect when it is the Holy Spirit within us who actually wields it.

You will recall that the perfect pattern of how to use the sword of the Spirit is provided by the encounter of Jesus with Satan at the time of His temptation in the wilderness. Three times Satan approached Jesus with a temptation and each time Jesus drove him back with the same phrase: "It is written" (Matthew 4:4, 7, 10). Jesus used no other weapon but the *rhema*—the spoken word of the Lord. God has made the same weapon available to each Christian.

It is important, however, to bear two things in mind. First, Jesus had already been "filled with the Holy Spirit" (Luke 4:1). It was the Holy Spirit in Jesus that directed Him in the use of the sword.

Second, Jesus—like every Jewish boy of His day—had memorized long passages of Scripture. When Satan confronted Him, He did not need to consult a concordance or go to a library. He had already stored up the Scriptures in His memory. Surely we today need to do that just as much as Jesus did!

7. All Prayer

This seventh weapon is not listed in exactly the same way as the previous six, but it is definitely needed to make the equipment of the Christian soldier complete. Of the previous six items, only the last one—the sword of the Spirit—is a weapon of attack, and even the sword is effective only as far as a soldier's arm can reach.

But this seventh weapon of *all prayer* is subject to no such limitations. We may fairly call it our ICBM—our *intercontinental ballistic missile*. Focused prayer, directed by the Holy Spirit, can reach across continents and oceans and strike with unerring accuracy at any target assigned to it. Undoubtedly, it is the most powerful and the most effective of all the weapons in the Christian arsenal.

Like the sword previously mentioned, this weapon of *all prayer* depends on the Holy Spirit for its effectiveness. It must be prayed "in the Spirit" (Ephesians 6:18). God does not commit such a weapon to Christians who are guided only by their carnal desires and emotions.

All prayer includes many different kinds of prayer—such as those listed in 1 Timothy 2:1: supplications, prayers, intercessions and giving of thanks. It is not a solo instrument to be played by one Christian on his own. Rather it is produced by an orchestra of many instruments blended together in harmony by the Holy Spirit.

Sometimes it takes apparently insurmountable obstacles to provoke this kind of prayer. In Acts 4:15–18 we read that the apostles were confronted with a satanic strategy that could have put a stop to all further evangelistic activity. The Jewish council, which was the supreme religious authority of the Jewish people, officially commanded the apostles "not to speak at all nor teach in the name of Jesus."

The opponents of the Gospel were perceptive enough to recognize the unique importance of the name of Jesus. The entire effectiveness of the Gospel was dependent on it. As Peter himself had declared to the council: "Nor is there salvation in any other, for there is no other name under heaven given among men by which we must be saved" (Acts 4:12). By this decree of the council, Satan had built a "stronghold" that would have prevented all further progress of the Gospel or growth of the infant Church.

Confronted with this satanic scheme, all the believers came together to seek God's help. Blended together into an orchestra, they cried out to the Lord for His intervention. God responded with such a demonstration of His power that "the place where they were assembled together was shaken; and they were all filled with the Holy Spirit, and they spoke the word of God with boldness" (Acts 4:31). The weapon of *all prayer* had demolished Satan's stronghold.

In many parts of the world today Satan has built up obstacles and opposition to the progress of the Gospel which resist all normal evangelistic methods. It is time for the Church to deploy its most powerful weapon: the weapon of *all prayer*.

20

The Climax of the Conflict

Confronted by the scriptural revelation of the rebellion of Satan and his angels against God, we might be tempted to exclaim: "Well, couldn't God have crushed that rebellion on the spot and sent Satan and all his angels to the lake of fire, where they belong?"

Certainly God could have done that, but He chose not to. In His inscrutable wisdom God chose to make Satan in his rebellion an instrument that He could use for purposes of His own. It was C. T. Studd, the English cricketer turned missionary, who remarked: "God has used Satan almost more than any other created being."

It is a principle of God's dealings with us that our relationships with Him are not secure until we have passed through certain tests that He has appointed. This applies to both angels and human beings. Untested relationships are like unrefined gold. They are not acceptable in heaven.

For this reason Jesus said to the Christians in Laodicea: "I counsel you to buy from Me gold refined in the fire" (Revelation 3:18). In other words, "Your claim to be My people is not valid until you have passed the test." Gold of that quality is not cheap. We have to *buy* it. There is a price to pay!

Satan the Tester

One main instrument that God uses to test us is Satan. Twice in Scripture he is called "the tempter" (see Matthew 4:3; 1 Thessalonians 3:5). This could more literally be translated *the tester*.

In the first instance God used Satan as His tester among the angels in heaven. Only those angels who refused to join Satan in his rebellion passed the test. Three times in reference to the return of Christ in glory and the judgments He will carry out, the Scripture states that He will be accompanied by the *holy* angels (see Matthew 25:31; Mark 8:38; Luke 9:26). These angels are distinguished from those who joined Satan in his rebellion and thus lost their holiness.

God also uses Satan to test humanity. This began with the first human beings—Adam and Eve. God placed them in the garden with one simple negative command: *not* to eat of the fruit of the tree of the knowledge of good and evil. Then Satan made his way into the garden and tempted them to do the one thing God had forbidden. When they yielded to this temptation, God pronounced judgment on all three of them. Satan had played his allotted role as the *tester*, but Adam and Eve had failed in their test. For this they alone were responsible.

Even in the life of Jesus Himself, Satan was permitted to play the role of tester. After Jesus had fasted forty days in the wilderness, the tempter (tester) came to Him and subjected Him to three successive temptations, or tests (see

Matthew 4:1–11). But where the first Adam had failed, the last Adam prevailed. He passed all three tests victoriously and Satan had to retreat.

Three and a half years later the tester was again released against Jesus. First of all, Satan entered into Judas Iscariot and used him to betray Jesus (see Luke 22:3). Then Satan stirred up a multitude of ungodly men to demand the crucifixion of Jesus. Once again, Jesus passed the test. He willingly laid down His life as a sacrifice for the sins of all humanity.

But it was here that the unsearchable wisdom of God reached its climax. The atoning death of Jesus on the cross canceled all of Satan's claims on fallen humanity. Satan's apparent victory became the cause of his irrevocable defeat.

From Slaves to Conquerors

Yet God still has one more way in which to use Satan as a demonstration of His own unfathomable wisdom. Satan tempted humanity into rebellion against God and thus made us his slaves. But through the atoning sacrifice of Jesus on the cross, God not only saved us from our sins and made us heirs of His Kingdom, but He actually made us instruments through which He will inflict final defeat on Satan.

John describes this war—still in the future—that finally puts an end to Satan's kingdom of rebellious angels in the heavenly places:

> And war broke out in heaven: Michael and his angels fought with the dragon; and the dragon and his angels fought, but they did not prevail, nor was a place found for them in heaven any longer. So the great dragon was cast out, that serpent of old, called the Devil and Satan, who deceives the whole world; he was cast to the earth, and his angels were cast out with him. Then I heard a loud voice saying

in heaven, "Now salvation, and strength, and the kingdom of our God, and the power of His Christ have come, for the accuser of our brethren, who accused them before our God day and night, has been cast down. And they overcame him by the blood of the Lamb and by the word of their testimony, and they did not love their lives to the death."

Revelation 12:7–11

This account brings out some extremely important facts:

1. Up to the time of the events here described, Satan and his angels continue to maintain their kingdom in the heavenly places.
2. When the voice in heaven speaks of "our brethren," it is referring to the believers on earth.
3. Satan and his angels are not driven out until they have been defeated by a combined force of God's angels in the heavenly places and the believers on earth.

This points to an amazing climax to the conflict: "*They* [the believers on earth] *overcame him* [Satan]." It is the redeemed believers on earth who are responsible for the final eviction of Satan from the heavenly places where he has maintained his kingdom. Satan's victims have finally become his conquerors. Only God could have planned that!

The battle is fought out with spiritual weapons. Satan's main weapon is *guilt*. That is why *he accuses us before God day and night*. He reminds God of all the sins we have committed. His purpose is to emphasize our guilt continually. If we are indeed guilty, then we have no power against him and no right to take his place in heaven.

Our victory will come only as we avail ourselves of the most powerful of all the weapons that God has put at our disposal: *the blood of the Lamb and the word of our testimony*. The blood of the Lamb affirms the all-sufficient sacrifice that Jesus offered on the cross on our behalf. "For by one offering [sac-

rifice] *He has perfected forever* [us] who are being sanctified"
(Hebrews 10:14, emphasis added). The sacrifice of Jesus on
our behalf is forever sufficient. Nothing need ever be added
to it and nothing can ever be taken from it. The last utterance
of Jesus on the cross was "It is finished!" (John 19:30). It is
completely complete and perfectly perfect.

The Pattern of the Passover

The provision that God has made for us in this end-time
conflict with Satan was prophetically foreshadowed in the
ordinances of the Passover through which God delivered
Israel from her slavery in Egypt. The lamb to be sacrificed
in the ceremony foreshadows Jesus "the Lamb of God."

It was the responsibility of the head of every Israelite
family to select and to slay the lamb and then to catch its
blood in a basin. But his task was not yet complete. The
blood in the basin did not protect any Israelite. The blood
had to be transferred from the basin and smeared on the
lintel and the two doorposts of every Israelite home. God's
promise was: "When I see the blood, I will pass over you"
(Exodus 12:13), that is, "My judgment will not come upon
you."

There was, therefore, one further essential element in the
Passover ceremony: a plant called hyssop, which grows
profusely over most of the Middle East. The head of every
family had to pluck a bunch of hyssop, dip it in the blood in
the basin and then sprinkle it on the lintel and the two doorposts of his home. Only then was that home protected.

How does this apply to the sacrifice of Jesus on the cross
when He poured out His lifeblood on our behalf? To borrow
a picture from the Passover ceremony, the blood is now in
the basin. But the blood in the basin protects no one. It has
to be transferred from the basin to the place where each
of us lives.

In the Passover ceremony it was the hyssop that applied the blood where it was needed. What is there in our lives that corresponds to the hyssop? How can we apply the blood of Jesus where we need it?

The answer is provided in Revelation 12:11: "They [the believers on earth] overcame him [Satan] by the blood of the Lamb and *by the word of their testimony*" (emphasis added). It is our testimony that does for us what the hyssop did for the Israelites. It is when we testify personally to what the blood of Jesus does for us that we can claim all the benefits that God has provided for us through the sacrifice of Jesus on the cross. Our bold, continuing personal testimony becomes the hyssop that applies the blood of Jesus to our lives.

We need to remember, however, that Satan has access to the Bible. He is familiar with the purposes of God revealed in Scripture. He knows that God intends to make the believers on earth one main instrument of his final defeat. His strategy, therefore, is to paralyze us with a sense of our guilt, to make us feel totally unworthy and inadequate. For this purpose he accuses us "before our God day and night" (Revelation 12:10).

We may ask: Why does God not silence Satan's accusations? The answer is that God will not do for us what He has given us the means to do for ourselves. He has provided for us spiritual weapons by which we can overcome every charge that Satan may bring against us. To every accusation of Satan we can respond that the blood of Jesus shed on the cross has provided a full and perfect propitiation. Therefore we are *not guilty*!

A Manual for End-Time Soldiers

In an earthly army a soldier who is enlisted is provided with appropriate weapons and then he receives training to make him proficient in their use. It is imperative for us as soldiers in the Lord's end-time army that we, too, become proficient in the use of the weapons that God has provided: the blood of the Lamb and the word of our testimony. We must learn how to testify appropriately concerning each provision made for us through the blood of Jesus.

I outline below a "training manual" on how to appropriate the various provisions made for us through the blood of Jesus. If you will familiarize yourself with the passages of Scripture—or, better still, commit them to memory—you will be prepared to take part in the vast spiritual conflict with which the present age will close.

> We overcome Satan when we testify personally to what the Word of God says the blood of Jesus does for us (see Revelation 12:11).
>
> Through the blood of Jesus, I am redeemed out of the hand of the devil (see Ephesians 1:7).
>
> Through the blood of Jesus, all my sins are forgiven (see 1 John 1:9).
>
> Through the blood of Jesus, I am continually being cleansed from all sin (see 1 John 1:7).
>
> Through the blood of Jesus I am justified, made righteous, just as if I'd never sinned (see Romans 5:9).
>
> Through the blood of Jesus, I am sanctified, made holy, set apart to God (see Hebrews 13:12).
>
> Through the blood of Jesus, I have boldness to enter into the presence of God (see Hebrews 10:19).
>
> The blood of Jesus cries out continually to God in heaven on my behalf (see Hebrews 12:24).

One Final Requirement

Revelation 12:11 closes with one distinguishing characteristic of all those who emerge victorious from this conflict: *"They did not love their lives to the death."*

How shall we apply this to ourselves? It means that for us it is more important to do the will of God than to stay alive. If we should ever find ourselves in a situation where to obey God will cost us our lives, then we will obey God.

Probably not all of us will actually have to make this clear-cut choice. But the decisive issue is our commitment. This imparts a quality to our testimony that makes it a weapon against which Satan has no defense. We each need, therefore, to confront ourselves with this question: *Can I truthfully say of myself that I do not love my life to the death?*

Part 4

Enduring to the End

21

Humanism: Forerunner for Antichrist

For we are not fighting against people made of flesh and blood, but against persons without bodies—the evil rulers of the unseen world, those mighty satanic beings and great evil princes of darkness who rule this world; and against huge numbers of wicked spirits in the spirit world.

Ephesians 6:12, TLB

As followers of Jesus Christ, we find ourselves caught up in a conflict that spans both heaven and earth. The forces that confront us are "persons without bodies"—evil spiritual powers in the unseen realm that oppose all true righteousness and seek to establish Satan's dominion over the whole world.

Our responsibility in this conflict is unique, because Christ has committed to us alone the spiritual insight and weapons that can give us victory. The governments and the armies of this world, operating solely in the natural plane, have no understanding of the conflict and no power to deal with the satanic forces in the heavenlies. On the contrary, without realizing it, they themselves are manipulated and controlled by those forces.

One essential requirement for victory is to identify the nature of the forces that are at work in any given situation. In recent months as I have been meditating on developments in the world—and especially in the United States and Israel—I believe that God has shown me the identity of the evil, deceptive power that Satan plans to use to consummate his purposes for the end of this age. It is *humanism*.

I had always thought of humanism as a comparatively harmless error. When I consulted a dictionary, I was taken aback by its definition: "The denial of any power or moral value superior to that of humanity; the rejection of religion in favor of a belief in the advancement of humanity by its own efforts."

I realized that humanism is not spiritually neutral. On the contrary, it is a deliberate denial and rejection of God's power and authority. It is an anti-religious religion. For this reason, it can be—and often is—taught in educational systems, such as those in America, that prohibit the teaching of religion in its usual sense.

I decided to trace humanism back through history, starting with Nebuchadnezzar's dream of an image with a head of gold, chest and arms of silver, belly and thighs of bronze, and legs of iron. Daniel interpreted this as foreshowing four Gentile empires that would arise in succession. The head was Babylon; the chest and arms were Media-Persia; the belly and thighs were Greece; the legs were Rome (see Daniel 2:31–40).

One key factor was impressed upon me: The reproductive organs were in the area identified with Greece. With my background in Greek philosophy, this became particularly vivid to me. I realized that it was Greece—more than any of the other empires—that, through its philosophy, reproduced itself in subsequent cultures.

Two of the early Greek philosophers of whom we have a record are Heraclitus and Protagoras. Three of their surviving sayings are: "All things flow"; "You can never step twice into the same river"; and "Man is the measure of all things." It is amazing how these three sayings sum up the essence of humanism. They assert that everything is relative; there are no moral or legal absolutes; and man is the highest authority in the universe.

It is outside the scope of this study to analyze how this thinking has molded, first, the concepts of Europe, and then, through Europe, the concepts of contemporary "civilization." The Greeks idolized the human mind. Aristotle's concept of God was a perfect mind contemplating itself—because nothing less was worthy of its contemplation. Out of this the whole philosophy of rationalism has developed.

In addition to philosophy, another main element of Greek culture was its emphasis on athletic contests. Their Olympic Games represented what was, in fact, an idolatry of athletic prowess, which has come back to life in the present century. The most widely viewed TV programs today are the great international sporting contests.

The Greeks also tended to downgrade the marriage relationship between a man and a woman, and to view a homosexual relationship between two men as being more "intellectually fulfilling." In their statuary, the idealized male form was usually presented naked, whereas the female was draped with some form of robe.

The so-called gods of Greece exhibited all the moral failings of humanity: lust, immorality, jealousy, vindictiveness and deception—a complete absence, in fact, of any binding moral code. This left man free to be his own god, and to establish his own moral code. After all, no people can be expected to live above the level of its own gods.

177

All these effects of Greek humanism have been increasingly evident in our Western culture. There is an open and deliberate rejection of God's righteous laws and of the covenants He made with man, first through Moses and then through Jesus Christ. It has been demonstrated that, carried to its ultimate conclusion, humanism will believe anything but the Truth and will tolerate anything but righteousness.

This exaltation of man is the force that will finally give rise to the Antichrist, whose name is "the number of a man" (see Revelation 13:18), the *man* of sin (lawlessness), who opposes and exalts himself above everything that is called God or is worshiped, and even sets himself up in God's temple, proclaiming himself to be God (see 2 Thessalonians 2:3–4).

Scripture reveals that he will bring under his dominion all who have refused the love of the truth. For this reason, God will send them a powerful delusion so that they will believe *the lie*—the original lie, that is, with which Satan deceived our first parents: "You will be like God" or "like gods." This exaltation of man in the place of God will usher in the "great tribulation"—a period of worldwide agony so terrible that it will exceed even the Holocaust of 1939–1945 (see Matthew 24:21–22).

Before this final period of tribulation, however, God still has tremendous purposes to work out for both Israel and the Church. A harvest of mercy will precede the harvest of judgment. God's preparation for this is revealed in Zechariah 9:13: "I will stir up your sons, O Zion, against your sons, O Greece" (NASB).

The "sons of Greece" are those who embrace the deception of humanism. The "sons of Zion" are those who take their stand upon the infallible Word of God, embracing both its promises and its covenants. They will be drawn both from natural Israel and from the professing Church. Of them it will be said, "They overcame him [Satan] by the blood of the Lamb and by the word of their testimony, and they did not love their lives to the death" (Revelation 12:11). They will be people with one overriding priority; to do the will of God will be more important to them than to hold on to life itself.

Numerically, we are vastly outnumbered by the forces of humanism. Nevertheless, we can take courage from the example of Asa, king of Judah. Facing an invasion by an overwhelmingly superior army, his prayer of desperation turned sure defeat into total victory. For us today, his prayer provides a wonderful pattern with which to counter the self-exalting forces of humanism.

> "LORD, there is no one like you to help the powerless against the mighty. Help us, O LORD our God, for we rely on you, and in your name we have come against this vast army. O LORD, you are our God; *do not let man prevail against you.*"
>
> 2 Chronicles 14:11, NIV, emphasis added

Again we must ask ourselves: Am I ready to take my stand as one of the sons of Zion?

22

Will Satan Ever Be Reconciled to God?

We have learned that, as Christians in today's world, we are often unaware that we are being subjected to a continuous inaudible bombardment by a philosophy called *humanism*. This presents man as the ultimate arbiter of moral or spiritual truth and promises a final and all-embracing reconciliation between God and all the forces of evil. This reconciliation, it is claimed, will include Satan himself and all the fallen angels and demons as well as any others who are presently at enmity with God. There is no place left for the absolute, unending punishment of any created being.

With its emphasis on reconciliation, this doctrine has a strong appeal for sincere and well-meaning Christians. Yet, it is based on a distortion of Scripture. One text commonly proposed, for instance, is Colossians 1:19–20, which reads:

> For it pleased the Father that in Him [Christ] all the fullness
> should dwell, and by Him to reconcile all things to Himself,
> by Him, whether things on earth or things in heaven, having
> made peace through the blood of His cross.

The emphasis is placed by this doctrine on the central phrase, "by Him *to reconcile all things to Himself.*" We notice, however, that the phrase "all things" is immediately qualified by the next phrase "whether things on earth or things in heaven." Thus, the reconciliation here spoken of *extends only to those things that are on earth or in heaven.*

This qualification becomes significant when we examine the description of the last great judgment of God given in Revelation 20:7–15. In verse 11 we are told that "the earth and the heaven fled away" from God's presence. Then, in verse 15 we are told that "anyone not found written in the Book of Life was cast into the lake of fire." This indicates that, even after heaven and earth have fled away, the lake of fire continues to exist in its own place. That is to say, the lake of fire is not located in either earth or heaven, and is therefore *not included in the scope of the reconciliation spoken of in Colossians 1:20.* Thus, the statement in Colossians 1:20 gives no reason to claim that those who are consigned to the lake of fire will ever thereafter be reconciled to God. In other words, the lake of fire is outside the boundary of reconciliation.

How Long Is "Eternal"?

Another line of argument designed to disprove any form of final, unending punishment is based on an interpretation of the Greek adjective *aionios,* which is normally translated "eternal" or "everlasting." It is claimed that this Greek adjective is derived from the Greek noun *aion,* meaning an "age" (eon), and that the adjective, therefore, has the meaning "belonging to, or extending throughout, an age." In other words, that which is called *aionios* does not extend through all ages, but only through one age.

This interpretation, for example, is applied to the words of Jesus: "And they [the wicked] will go away into *eternal* punishment, but the righteous into *eternal* life" (Matthew 25:46, RSV, emphasis added). Proponents of this idea claim that the phrase "eternal punishment" does not mean absolute, unending punishment, but merely punishment that lasts for an age (and, by implication, is terminated after that). If that were the case, however, intellectual honesty would demand that "eternal life" be interpreted in the same way. Does anyone sincerely believe that this is what Jesus meant?

On the contrary, this verse surely supplies proof that the adjective *aionios* does not mean merely "that which endures for an age," but rather "from age to age" or "to all ages." This meaning is the same whether the adjective is applied to *life* or to *punishment*.

This is confirmed by the use of another phrase that occurs in the Greek New Testament, namely: *eis* [*tous*] *aionas ton aionon*—that is, "unto [the] ages of ages." This phrase occurs approximately twenty times in the Greek New Testament, and is normally translated "forever and ever." The Greek language cannot produce any phrase that more strongly expresses that which endures for all ages, absolutely without end.

The same phrase is also used in Revelation 20:10, where it says of the devil, the beast and the false prophet, "They will be tormented day and night *forever and ever*" (emphasis added). There is no way to express more emphatically that their punishment will be totally and absolutely unending.

The Only Basis of Reconciliation

Those who speak of Satan being reconciled to God do not understand the scriptural basis of reconciliation.

Peter tells us: "The Lord . . . is longsuffering toward us, not willing that any should perish but that all should come to repentance" (2 Peter 3:9). Notice that God's longsuffering is toward "us," the human race. Notice also the great, unvarying condition upon which alone God's mercy and reconciliation are offered: repentance. Repentance signifies humble acknowledgment of wrongdoing, total turning away from wrongdoing, and sincere and unreserved submission to God. Where there is no repentance, there can be no reconciliation.

It is possible for the will of a created being to be so set in rebellion that there is thereafter no possibility of its being changed. In such a case, repentance is no longer possible. In Hebrews 12:17 we are told of Esau that "afterward, when he wanted to inherit the blessing, he was rejected, for he found no place for repentance." More literally, "he found no way to change his mind." So far as the birthright was concerned, Esau had made an irrevocable decision. There was, therefore, no way back into the blessing that he had forfeited.

The same stands eternally true of Satan and his angels. In their initial rebellion against God, in the full light and knowledge of eternity, they made an irrevocable, irreversible commitment. Their wills are set forever in eternal, irreconcilable enmity and opposition to Almighty God. Satan is incapable of repentance; therefore, there is for him no possibility of reconciliation.

Christ as Substitute for Men, Not Angels

Scripture makes it clear that the propitiatory sacrifice of Christ was made solely on behalf of the human race. Jesus is the "Lamb of God who takes away the sin of the world!" (John 1:29). He is "the propitiation for our sins, and not for ours only but also for the whole world" (1 John 2:2).

In each case the English word *world* translates the Greek word *kosmos*. A thorough examination will show that this Greek word *kosmos*, throughout the New Testament, is used solely and exclusively of this earth and of the human race upon it.

Three passages from the New Testament may be cited in confirmation of this. In Romans 5:12, Paul says that "through one man sin entered the world [*kosmos*]." That *one man* was, of course, Adam. Sin had already been committed in heaven by Satan and his angels, but that was *outside the world*. Sin *in the world* began with the human race upon earth. Peter tells us, concerning the judgment of God upon the human race in the days of Noah, that God "did not spare the ancient world, but saved Noah" (2 Peter 2:5) and that "the world that then existed perished, being flooded with water" (2 Peter 3:6). In both these cases, "the world" refers to the human race upon earth. Satan and his fallen angels are not included.

It follows that when Jesus atoned by His death on the cross for the sins of "the world," He atoned for the human race upon the earth, but not for Satan and his angels. This is in line with the revelation given in Hebrews:

> Since therefore the children share in flesh and blood, he himself [Jesus] likewise partook of the same nature, that through death he might destroy him who has the power of death, that is, the devil. . . . For surely it is not with angels that he is concerned but with the descendants of Abraham.
>
> Hebrews 2:14, 16, RSV

Jesus became, by His fleshly nature, a descendant of Abraham—and thus also of Adam. He was "the last Adam" (1 Corinthians 15:45). He became on the cross the atoning substitute for the whole Adamic race. But He did not take on angelic nature, and He did not become a substitute for angels. There is, therefore, no basis in divine justice for the offer of pardon to angels. In fact, the very purpose of the death of Jesus on the cross was not to save the devil but, on the contrary, to "destroy . . . the devil" (Hebrews 2:14). What could be clearer than that?

For this reason, Christ—returned in glory at the close of this age—is revealed as saying to the "goats" on His left hand: "Depart from Me, you cursed, into the everlasting fire prepared for the devil and his angels" (Matthew 25:41). This everlasting fire—also called Gehenna, or the lake of fire—was "prepared for the devil and his angels." This is their sure, inevitable, eternal destination. This place of punishment, however, was not prepared for the human race. Human beings do not need to go there. If they will repent and submit to God, God will spare them. For them there is an alternative—if they will accept it. But for Satan and his angels there is no alternative.

Satan's Advocates Are God's Enemies

In this spiritual realm there is no neutrality. Jesus said: "He who is not with Me is against Me" (Matthew 12:30). There are only two possible attitudes: submission to God or opposition to God. Human beings who, through repentance, submit themselves to God, are spared from the lake of fire. All others, who do not thus submit, are in opposition to God. They necessarily associate themselves with the devil and his angels. Because of this association, they are condemned to the same destination—the lake of fire. For all who once enter this lake of fire—whether angels or men—there is no way back. It is "forever and ever."

Herein lies the subtle danger of this doctrine of "reconciliation" for those who profess to be Christians. In the Scriptures, God clearly states two things. First, God is absolutely just and impartial. Second, God has condemned the devil and his angels to the punishment of everlasting fire. Any person who questions the second of these two statements automatically questions the first also.

Think of it like this. The picture presented in Scripture of God's nature and dealings with man is like a coin. It has two opposite sides, which together make up the complete coin. These two sides are presented by Paul: "Therefore consider the goodness and severity of God" (Romans 11:22). Here are the two sides: *goodness* and *severity*. On the one hand, mercy and grace; on the other hand, wrath and judgment.

To efface one side of a coin renders it incomplete and valueless. So it is with the picture of God presented in the Bible. To speak always of goodness, but never of severity—to speak always of mercy and grace, but never of wrath and judgment—this is to efface one side of the coin, and to render the Bible's picture of God incomplete and valueless. Those who speak like this are unfaithful to God, and unfair to men. In so doing, they misrepresent God and mislead men.

Do you see how vital it is to understand the danger of this doctrine? Anyone who denies that the devil is condemned to everlasting fire, automatically repudiates both the truth and the justice of God. By this subtle deception, Satan has tricked well-meaning Christians into taking sides with him against God. No one can, at the same time, be the advocate of Satan and the friend of God.

Has this attitude crept into your heart? If so, you must change your mind. Renounce your association with the devil. Lay down your opposition to God. Humble yourself. Submit yourself to the truth and the justice of God. In so doing, you open the way for God to restore to you His grace, mercy and peace. Consider the words of David:

> Do not I hate them, O LORD, who hate You?
> And do I not loathe those who rise up against You?
> I hate them with perfect hatred;
> I count them my enemies.

Search me, O God, and know my heart;
Try me, and know my anxieties;
And see if there is any wicked way in me,
And lead me in the way everlasting.

Psalm 139:21–24

Make this confession of David your confession concerning Satan and his angels. Ask the Lord to search your heart. Renounce every wicked way. Return to the way everlasting. It is a requirement of those who would endure.

23

Anti-Semitism
and Jesus' Return

A Roman Catholic historian has given a brief but vivid summation of 2,300 years of continuous anti-Semitism:

> As the historian of anti-Semitism looks back over the millennia of horrors he has recorded, an inescapable conclusion emerges: Anti-Semitism is the longest and deepest hatred of human history. Other hatreds may have surpassed it in intensity for a historical moment, but all in their turn have assumed—or presently commence to assume—their proper place in the dustbin of history. What other hatred has endured some twenty-three centuries and survived a genocide of 6,000,000 of its victims in its twenty-third century of existence only to find itself still intact and rich in potential for many more years of life? The very magnitude of the record, seen as a whole, cries out for explanation.

How did this amalgam of undying hatred and oppression come to be? What is it essentially? Who or what was responsible for it?

In his book *The Anguish of the Jews* (Paulist Press, 1985), Michael Flannery goes on to offer his own explanation of anti-Semitism. His remarks are illuminating and helpful, as are other explanations of anti-Semitism representing a variety of different approaches—theological, philosophical, sociological, economic. None, however, has ever seemed an adequate explanation.

In 1946, I discussed this question with my first Hebrew teacher, Mr. Ben Zion Segal, who was the secretary of the newly established Hebrew University—located at the time on Mount Scopus, Jerusalem. Mr. Segal believed that the problem of anti-Semitism was basically sociological: The Jews were always an alien minority with a distinctive culture of their own, out of harmony with the culture of the Gentile nations that harbored them. Once the Jews got a state of their own—which actually happened two years later—this would resolve the basic cause of anti-Semitism.

To this I replied: "If you are correct that the basic cause of anti-Semitism is sociological, then the establishment of a Jewish state should go a long way toward resolving the problem. But if—as I believe—the basic cause is spiritual, the establishment of a Jewish state will not resolve the problem, but will intensify it by providing it with one obvious focus: the newly established Jewish state."

Looking back now, I have to say—regretfully—that I believe history has proved me right. The establishment of the State of Israel has merely provided a more "politically correct" name—"anti-Zionism" in place of "anti-Semitism." If anything, the virulence has increased.

Even if we rightly identify the basic cause of anti-Semitism as spiritual, however, this still does not lay bare the root. Quite recently, however, without any conscious searching on my part, I received two successive flashes of inspiration from the Scriptures that I believe do trace anti-Semitism to its root.

While I was preaching in our local church in Jerusalem, quite unexpectedly I heard myself say, "Anti-Semitism can be summed up in one word—*Messiah!*"

At that moment I understood that from its beginning anti-Semitism had one source—Satan—who was motivated by the knowledge that the One who was to be his conqueror, the Messiah, would come through a people that would be specially prepared by God. This people would have one distinctive feature: The Messiah would be able to set an example of obedience to his earthly parents without dishonoring his heavenly Father by any form of idolatry. Molded by God through many centuries, the Jewish people alone fulfilled this requirement.

Then I saw how, from the birth of Israel as a nation onward, Satan had unceasingly sought to do two things: to entice them into idolatry, and, if that failed, to completely destroy them as a nation. Satan's attempts to entice Israel into idolatry are a recurring feature of their national history.

History also records two main attempts of Satan to destroy Israel as a nation. In Egypt, Pharaoh ordered the murder of all their male babies. If this had been carried through, it would have effectively terminated their existence as a nation. Later, Haman came very close to carrying through a decree for the extermination of all the Jews in the Persian Empire—which was in effect all the Jews alive at that time.

In the second century B.C., Antiochus Epiphane, the dictator of Syria, attempted by force of arms to compel the Jews to renounce their unique destiny as a nation and to merge into the idolatrous culture of the surrounding Greek empire. Only the courageous resistance of the Maccabees foiled his attempt and ensured that a century and a half later there was a Jewish nation to which Jesus could be born as Messiah.

Through His sacrificial death on the cross Jesus fulfilled the purpose for which He came. As the representative of Israel and all nations, He satisfied the requirements of God's justice on our behalf and thus canceled all Satan's claims against us. By this He imposed upon Satan a total, eternal, irrevocable defeat. The full outworking of this defeat, however, will only be consummated *at the Second Coming of Jesus.*

Satan, who pays more attention to biblical prophecy than many preachers, is fully aware of all this. Until Jesus returns, Satan knows that he will remain free to continue all his evil activities and to present himself as "the god of this age" (2 Corinthians 4:4).

There is, therefore, one event that Satan fears more than all others and that he opposes by every means in his power: the return of Jesus in power and glory to establish His Kingdom and to banish Satan from the earth. The opposition of Satan to the return of Jesus is the unseen force behind many of the conflicts and pressures in the contemporary world.

In His final prophetic discourses in Jerusalem, Jesus pinpointed two events that must precede His return to earth. First, He said, "And this gospel of the kingdom will be preached in all the world as a witness to all the nations, *and then the end will come*" (Matthew 24:14, emphasis added). Then, at the close of His earthly ministry, Jesus gave His disciples an explicit order: "Go into all the world and preach the gospel to every creature" (Mark 16:15); "Go therefore and make disciples of all the nations" (Matthew 28:19).

Jesus has never canceled this order. It is still in force. He will not return until His disciples have carried it out. Satan, therefore, uses every means in his power to divert the Church from completing its task. The longer the Church delays, the longer Satan retains his liberty.

Just previously, however, Jesus had said this to the Jews in Jerusalem: "See! Your house [that is, the Temple] is left

191

to you desolate; for I say to you, you shall see Me no more till you say, 'Blessed is He who comes in the name of the LORD!'" (Matthew 23:38–39).

The way in which the Lord will prepare the hearts of the Jews for this is predicted in Zechariah 12:10:

> "And I will pour on the house of David and on the inhabitants of Jerusalem the Spirit of grace and supplication; then they will look on Me whom they pierced. Yes, they will mourn for Him as one mourns for his only son, and grieve for Him as one grieves for a firstborn."

The Holy Spirit will move supernaturally on the hearts of the Jewish people to bring a revelation of their Messiah and anguished repentance for having rejected and crucified Him. Notice, however, that this description refers specifically to "the house of David and the inhabitants of Jerusalem." The restoration of the Jews to their own land and to the city of Jerusalem is an essential preliminary. Until this takes place, the defeat of Satan will not be finally consummated.

This, then, is the second condition that must be fulfilled before Jesus will return: The Jews must be regathered in their own land and in the city of Jerusalem, and their hearts must be prepared to acknowledge Jesus as Messiah. Just as surely as Jesus came the first time *through* the Jews, so surely He will come back the second time *to* the Jews.

This insight gave me an altogether new understanding of the worldwide furor and confusion concerning the situation in Israel. What else could explain the almost daily focus of the world media, of the United Nations and of the world's most powerful governments upon a tiny strip of land with a population of five million and an area about the size of the nation of Wales? There is no normal, political explanation for such a concentration of world forces upon a situation and a people that would normally be considered insignificant.

I also understood in a new light the revelation of the prophet Joel that at the close of this age God will judge all nations on the basis of their attitude toward the regathering of Israel in their own land:

"For behold, in those days and at that time,
When I bring back the captives of Judah and Jerusalem,
I will also gather all nations,
And bring them down to the Valley of Jehoshaphat;
And I will enter into judgment with them there
On account of My people, My heritage Israel,
Whom they have scattered among the nations;
They have also divided up My land."

Joel 3:1–2

The implications of these revelations are far-reaching and frightening. Our attitude toward the return of Jesus is revealed by two things: our concern for world evangelization and our concern for the reestablishment of the Jews in their own land.

If we are indifferent toward these two events, we are, in fact—whether we acknowledge it or not—indifferent to the return of Jesus. Probably there are many Christians who would give at least lip service to the urgency of world evangelism, but who are still blind to the significance of the restoration of Israel. Yet both alike are main themes of the prophetic Scriptures and of the words of Jesus Himself.

The issue of Israel's restoration goes much deeper than theology or intellectual understanding. Ultimately it is spiritual. The spirit that opposes the reestablishment of Israel is the spirit that opposes the return of Jesus. Though it may wear many disguises, it is the spirit of Satan himself.

Faced with these scriptural mandates, we each need to ask ourselves a decisive question: Am I sincerely committed to support by every legitimate means the task of world evangelization and the reestablishment of Israel as a nation in its own land? The answer we give will reveal our attitude toward the return of Jesus.

24

Learning from Balaam's Mistakes

At first glance it might seem that the story of Balaam, the soothsayer, recorded in Numbers 22–24 has no relevance for Christians engaging in spiritual battle. If that were the case, however, the writers of the New Testament probably would not have found relevance in his story. They refer to Balaam in three separate passages—always with a note of warning. Clearly, therefore, his story contains important lessons for us.

Balaam is a strange and intriguing personality—a baffling combination of supernatural spiritual gifts and corrupt character. Significantly, we see more and more ministries in today's Church with a similar combination of spiritual gifts and corrupt character.

The Story Begins

The story of Balaam opens with Israel finally encamped on the border of Canaan. Their presence inspired fear in Balak, the king of Moab, whose territory bordered the Israelites' encampment. Apparently he viewed the Israelites as a threat to his kingdom, although they had done nothing to justify his fear.

Feeling unable to confront Israel in battle, Balak decided to use spiritual weapons against them. He sent some of his princes—with a fee for divination in their hands—to call for Balaam to come and put a curse on Israel. As a "soothsayer" (fortune-teller or witch doctor), Balaam had the reputation of uttering blessings or curses with a powerful effect for good or evil.

Balaam came from Pethor in Mesopotamia. He was not an Israelite, yet he had direct personal knowledge of the one true God. At one point in this story, for instance, Balaam referred to "the Lord my God" (Numbers 22:18). The English form, "the Lord" (in capitals), is the accepted translation of the Hebrew sacred name of God, rendered either "Jehovah" or "Yahweh." Balaam knew God by His sacred name and called Him *my* God."

When the first emissaries of Balak arrived, God told Balaam not to go with them and not to curse Israel (see Numbers 22:12). Balaam obeyed.

Balak's response was to send a larger party of more honorable princes—with the promise of a much greater reward. This time the Lord gave Balaam permission to go on one condition: "If the men come to call you" (Numbers 22:20).

There is no record that the men did come to call Balaam again. Yet he went, and by his disobedience incurred the anger of the Lord, who opposed him on his journey and nearly killed him. Finally, however, the Lord released him to go, but set this condition: "Only the word that I speak to you, that you shall speak" (Numbers 22:35).

Balak welcomed Balaam and made the most elaborate preparations for him to curse Israel. But each time the result was exactly the opposite. Altogether, Balaam uttered four prophecies, which are among the most beautiful and powerful revelations in Scripture of God's irrevocable commitment to bless Israel.

Thwarted by God in his attempt to curse Israel, Balaam proposed a different strategy against her (see Numbers 31:16). If the Moabite women could entice the Israelites into idolatry and immorality, it would not be necessary to curse them. God Himself would bring judgment upon them. Balaam's second strategy succeeded and 24,000 Israelites perished under God's judgment (see Numbers 25:1–9).

In all of this Balaam displayed the most amazing inconsistency. More than once he had been explicitly forbidden to curse Israel. By supernatural revelation he had four times affirmed God's unchanging purpose to bless Israel and to judge her enemies. But he stubbornly persisted in cooperating with Balak, the enemy of Israel, and in plotting Israel's destruction. It was fitting that he should perish in the same judgment as the other enemies of Israel, executed by the Israelites together with the kings of Midian (see Numbers 31:8).

We are led to ask ourselves: What motive could be so powerful and compelling that it would cause Balaam to act in direct opposition to the revelation he had received from God—to his own ultimate destruction? Two writers of the New Testament answer this question.

Speaking of false teachers in the Church, Peter says: "They have forsaken the right way and gone astray, following the way of Balaam the son of Beor, who loved the wages of unrighteousness" (2 Peter 2:15).

Jude likewise, speaking of false teachers, says: "They . . . have run greedily in the error of Balaam for profit" (Jude 11).

The answer is clear. Balaam was tempted to his destruction by the love of money. For this he was willing to prostitute his marvelous spiritual gifts. Probably he was flattered, too, by the attention he received from King Balak and his princes. The love of money is closely associated with the desire for popularity and for power. All these evil lusts grow out of the selfsame soil: pride.

Lessons from Balaam

There are three important lessons that we need to learn from the story of Balaam.

First, Almighty God has made an irrevocable commitment to establish the Jews as His people forever. There is no power in the universe, human or satanic, that can ever annul this commitment. The Jews have many times been unfaithful to God, and He has brought severe judgments upon them, but their unfaithfulness can never annul God's faithfulness.

The initiative in this promise proceeds from God, not from men. The Jews did not choose God, but God chose the Jews.

I have a young friend, a former Muslim—let us call him Ali—who was supernaturally converted to Christ. After his conversion he began to bring up before God all his complaints against the Jews. Eventually God responded, "Ali, your problem is not with the Jews. It is with Me. I am the one who chose them." That young man now has a ministry winning Muslims for Christ and teaching them to pray for the Jews.

In Numbers 24:9, Balaam's prophecy reveals a decisive factor in the destiny of men and nations. Speaking to Israel, he says: "Blessed is he who blesses you, and cursed is he who curses you."

Individuals and nations alike determine their destiny—often without being aware of it—by their attitude toward the Jews. Those who bless are blessed and those who curse are cursed.

Second, one of Satan's strongest and most successful weapons against us is the love of money. This has been true from the earliest days of Christianity until now. A ministry accompanied by powerful supernatural signs—especially miracles of healing—can almost always become a means of making money.

Paul contrasted his own ministry with that of many of his Christian contemporaries with these words: "*Unlike so many, we do not peddle the word of God for profit*" (2 Corinthians 2:17, NIV, emphasis added). Even in Paul's day many Christians were using their ministries to make money!

Money in itself is not evil. It is not necessarily sinful to be wealthy. By nature, money is neutral. It can be used either for good or for evil. But when we begin to love money, then we are caught in Satan's snare. Paul used the most solemn language to warn us against this:

> But those who desire to be rich fall into temptation and a snare, and into many foolish and harmful lusts which drown men in destruction and perdition. For the love of money is a root of all kinds of evil, for which some have strayed from the faith in their greediness, and pierced themselves through with many sorrows.
>
> 1 Timothy 6:9–10

In my own ministry I have often taught on God's plan to prosper believers who are committed to the purposes of His Kingdom. Yet looking back now, I regret any occasion on which I taught this message without balancing it with Paul's warning here in 1 Timothy. In my mind's eye, I picture believers who have succumbed to the love of money as people who have taken a sharp, poisoned dagger and plunged it into their own flesh. Certainly this is what Balaam did.

Third, we need to understand the difference between spiritual gifts and spiritual fruit. Gifts represent ability, but fruit represents character. As we have learned, a gift comes through a single brief impartation, but fruit comes through a slow process of development. Receiving a spiritual gift does not, in itself, change a person's character. If a person was proud or unreliable or deceitful before receiving a spiritual gift, that person will still be proud or unreliable or deceitful after receiving it.

Receiving such a gift does, however, increase a person's responsibility, because it increases the influence he can have on others. It also carries with it a temptation to see "success" in the Christian life in terms of exercising spiritual gifts rather than in terms of developing a godly character. Paradoxical as it may seem, *the more gifts a person receives, the more attention he needs to pay to cultivating fruit.* When we pass from time to eternity, we will leave our gifts behind, but our character will be with us forever.

That Balaam had a clear vision of the blessed end that awaits the righteous is shown by his prayer: "Let me die the death of the righteous, and let my end be like his!" (Numbers 23:10). Yet Balaam's prayer was not granted. He was executed in God's judgment upon the Moabites, whose money had tempted him to align himself against God.

The fate of Balaam provides a graphic illustration of Jesus' teaching given in Matthew:

"Not everyone who says to Me, 'Lord, Lord,' shall enter the kingdom of heaven, but he who does the will of My Father in heaven. Many will say to Me in that day, 'Lord, Lord, have we not prophesied in Your name, cast out demons in Your name, and done many wonders in Your name?' And then I will declare to them, 'I never knew you; depart from Me, you who practice lawlessness!'"

Matthew 7:21–23

Simply stated, there is no substitute for obeying God. That alone is rule enough for a Christian soldier.

25

Preparing to Reign with Christ

Do you not know that the saints will judge the world?

1 Corinthians 6:2

God has a double purpose in redeeming us. On the negative side, it is to save us from hell—for which we should be eternally grateful. On the positive side, it is to prepare a people for Himself, who will share the throne with Christ.

Before you read any further, pause for a moment and consider what it means to you personally, as a Christian, that you should be preparing yourself to reign eternally with Christ. For our part, Ruth and I have found that the Holy Spirit is laying an ever-increasing emphasis on preparing for our destiny in eternity. Look at these promises:

"Assuredly I say to you, that in the regeneration, when the Son of Man sits on the throne of His glory, you who have followed Me will also sit on twelve thrones, judging the twelve tribes of Israel."

Matthew 19:28

"And he who overcomes, and keeps My works until the end, to him I will give power over the nations—'He shall rule them with a rod of iron; they shall be dashed to pieces like the potter's vessels.'"

Revelation 2:26–27

For this awesome responsibility of reigning with Christ we are required to make diligent preparation. It is not enough merely to claim to be "born again." The following are some main requirements.

1. Endurance

If we are to share Christ's exaltation, we must first share His death and then continue steadfast to the end through many trials.

"But you are those who have continued with Me in My trials. And I bestow upon you a kingdom, just as My Father bestowed one upon Me, that you may eat and drink at My table in My kingdom, and sit on thrones judging the twelve tribes of Israel."

Luke 22:28–30

At the Last Supper, Jesus honored the steadfastness of the Twelve by counting them worthy to reign with Him over Israel. (Note, Judas Iscariot by his treachery forfeited his right to a throne and it was given to another instead. See Acts 1:15–26.)

And those of us who continue today to endure as His disciples to the end? "For if we died with Him, we shall also live with Him. If we endure, we shall also reign with Him" (2 Timothy 2:11–12). We will continue more specifically with this requirement in the next two chapters.

2. Meekness, Poverty of Spirit

God does not offer His Kingdom to those who are arrogant or self-assertive, but only to those who recognize that in themselves they are totally unworthy of such honor. Hannah, the mother of Samuel, declared in her song of triumph: "He [God] raises the poor from the dust and lifts the beggar from the ash heap, to set them among princes and make them inherit the throne of glory" (1 Samuel 2:8).

A thousand years later, the Virgin Mary—in an even greater song of triumph—proclaimed the same truth: "He has put down the mighty from their thrones, and exalted the lowly" (Luke 1:52).

We also read: "Blessed are the poor in spirit, for theirs is the kingdom of heaven" (Matthew 5:3) and "Blessed are the meek, for they shall inherit the earth" (Matthew 5:5).

3. Purity

The people whom Christ acknowledged as His own are those whom He has redeemed from every lawless deed and purified for Himself: "Christ . . . gave Himself for us, that He might redeem us from every lawless deed and purify for Himself His own special people, zealous for good works" (Titus 2:13–14).

But there are two sides to this process of purification: one divine, the other human. The apostle John speaks of our hope of being transformed into Christ's likeness at His return, but then he adds: "And everyone who has this hope in Him purifies himself, just as He is pure" (1 John 3:3). Christ will only purify those who respond by purifying themselves. Furthermore, God has only one standard of purity: "just as He [Jesus] is pure."

Peter tells us how we may purify our souls: by "obeying the truth through the Spirit," resulting in "sincere love of the brethren" (1 Peter 1:22). The purified soul is a soul filled with love.

4. Love of the Truth

It was by deception that Satan enticed Adam and Eve into rebellion against God, and this has been his main weapon against humanity ever since. In Revelation he is called "that serpent of old . . . who deceives the whole world" (Revelation 12:9). And Paul warns in 2 Thessalonians 2:9–11 that this satanic tactic will find its ultimate expression in the Antichrist, who will deceive with lying signs and wonders all those who "did not receive the love of the truth" (2 Thessalonians 2:10).

Here, then, is our only protection: *to receive the love of the truth*. All who refuse this will not merely be deceived by Satan; God Himself will send them strong delusion.

Love of the truth is not mere conformity to a religious code, however "orthodox" it may be. Nor is it even reading your Bible and having a "quiet time" every day. It demands a total, unreserved commitment to believe and obey God's Word—one that rules out all forms of compromise.

In the time of Jesus, many Jews recognized that Jesus was the Messiah, but for fear of the religious authorities they did not acknowledge Him, "for they loved the praise of men more than the praise of God" (John 12:43). That is the essence of compromise. We each need to ask ourselves: Which means more to me—God's approval . . . or man's?

Solomon counsels, "Buy the truth, and do not sell it" (Proverbs 23:23). Truth is not obtained cheaply. It demands much time given to prayer and study of the Scriptures, followed by practical application in our daily lives. It must take priority over the many forms of cheap entertainment offered by our secular culture. It is a lifetime commitment.

We are also warned not to *sell* the truth. We can be tempted to purchase popularity at the price of truth by leaving out the "hard sayings" of Jesus and presenting a Gospel that demands no sacrifice but promises an easy way through life. Yet this belies the warning of Jesus: "Narrow is the gate and difficult is the way which leads to life, and there are few who find it" (Matthew 7:14).

If you are serious in your desire to share Christ's Kingdom with Him, let me suggest that you read carefully several times the Scriptures I have quoted above, and consider how each one applies to your own life. If the Holy Spirit shows you areas in which you fall short, ask His help to make the changes that are needed.

What will it take to succeed? Endurance.

26

Character That
Stands the Test

*E*ndurance. It is not a very popular word—nor one that is easily understood. Nonetheless, we cannot succeed in battle without it. I believe we are living in times when it is increasingly important that we understand what it means to endure.

The King James Version of the Bible was translated well over three hundred years ago, and the meaning of some English words has changed. Normally, the King James Version uses the word *patience* where today we would use *endurance*. And where we would talk about *patience*, the King James Version uses the word *longsuffering*. Patience or longsuffering is being willing to put up with irritating people, situations and circumstances without losing your temper—to remain composed and not fly off the handle. It is a valuable Christian virtue. I am well aware that I could use more of it myself. But when the King James Version uses the word *patience*, the modern equivalent is *endurance* or *perseverance*—those are the words that are used in most of the modern translations of the Bible. The verb form that the King James Version uses is usually "to endure."

On the Mount of Olives, Jesus gave a prophetic preview of the situation that would exist in the world immediately prior to His return. Many of the things that He spoke about we see manifested in the world today. My purpose in this chapter, however, is not to explore prophetic interpretations, but to focus on the one characteristic that Jesus said we are going to need to get through days like these. "And because lawlessness will abound, the love of many will grow cold. But he who endures to the end shall be saved" (Matthew 24:12–13).

Notice, there is a direct connection between lawlessness and lovelessness. When people become lawless, they become loveless. We often think of love as something free and spontaneous, something that requires no laws and no discipline. That is incorrect. Love and discipline go hand in hand. When discipline and law break down, love grows cold. The word for *love* in verse 12 is *agape*, which refers essentially to the love of Christians. Jesus is not talking about the love of the world growing cold, but the love of Christians growing cold.

In the midst of this terribly bleak climate—lawlessness abounding and love growing cold—Jesus says: "But he who endures to the end shall be saved." We have to endure to the end. The original Greek says, "He that has endured unto the end, it is he who will be saved."

In Mark's rendering of the Olivet Discourse you will notice this warning repeated:

"Now brother will betray brother to death, and a father his child; and children will rise up against parents and cause them to be put to death. And you will be hated by all for My name's sake. But he who endures to the end shall be saved."

Mark 13:12–13

This is a somber picture of rampant treachery and disloyalty within family relationships and toward Christians who will be hated by all. And then the admonition is the same: endure. We must hold out. Sometimes holding out is all God asks you to do—and it can be a full-time job.

I met a Swedish missionary who had worked in France for many years. He told me that he had visited a prison near Marseilles in the south of France where the French Huguenots (the Protestants of that time) had been imprisoned for their faith. Many of them went into the dungeon there and never came out alive. The missionary told of one prisoner who had engraved in the stone of the dungeon one single word: *résister*—the French word for *resist*. That was the message one believer left to the others who would follow him. Resist. Don't give in. Hold out. Endure. I believe that God is speaking that word to us today. I pray that God, through His Word, will put steel in your soul and give you a spiritual backbone if you do not already have one.

The Fruit of Tribulation

How do we continue to cultivate endurance? Here are some simple principles.

Therefore, having been justified by faith, we have peace with God through our Lord Jesus Christ, through whom also we have access by faith into this grace in which we stand, and rejoice in hope of the glory of God.

Romans 5:1–2

We rejoice because of what the future holds for us. But Paul goes on to say that not only do we rejoice in the light of the future, but we also rejoice in what the present offers, although it is very different. "And not only that, but we also glory in tribulations, knowing that tribulation produces perseverance; and perseverance, character; and character, hope" (verses 3–4).

Where verse 3 uses the word *glory*, the same word, as used in Greek, means "to rejoice, boast or exult." And why should we exult in tribulation? Because of what tribulation does. The New American Standard Bible says, "Tribulation brings about perseverance; and perseverance, proven character; and proven character, hope." Perseverance produces *proven* character in us. This is the heart of endurance—character that has stood the test. Look at verse 5: "Now hope does not disappoint, because the love of God has been poured out in our hearts by the Holy Spirit who was given to us."

Here we see that love is a matter of character. In essence, we are dealing with the forming of our character—the character of a soldier that endures to the end. We rejoice (boast, glory or exult) in tribulation because tribulation is the only thing that produces perseverance. And perseverance produces proven character. I know men with whom I have walked, shared hardship, opposition, misrepresentation and misunderstanding—even misunderstanding between them and me. But today, for me, their character is proven; I know I can trust them. In the midst of treachery and lawlessness, I want to know whom I can trust.

First of all, though, I want to be sure that I can be trusted. I am well aware of the daily pressures that tempt us to serve ourselves at others' expense. But I would be horribly ashamed if pressure could make me unfaithful or disloyal to those I am committed to in the Body of Christ.

Let's look at the first chapter of Colossians:

For this reason we also, since the day we heard it, do not
cease to pray for you, and to ask that you may be filled
with the knowledge of His will in all wisdom and spiritual
understanding; that you may walk worthy of the Lord,
fully pleasing Him, being fruitful in every good work and
increasing in the knowledge of God; strengthened with all
might, according to His glorious power, for all patience and
longsuffering with joy.

Colossians 1:9–11

Isn't it wonderful to know that God wants us to be filled
with the knowledge of His will in all wisdom and spiritual
understanding? Where Paul says, "that you may walk worthy
of the Lord," keep in mind that when we are filled with the
knowledge of God's will, it will affect the way we live. It will
even affect how we handle adversity. It is one thing to suffer
long; it is quite another thing to suffer long with *joyfulness*. It
takes endurance and strength to do it. Patience and endurance
are marks of strength; they are not marks of weakness.

One of the consistent themes of Hebrews is the danger
of going back on our profession of faith in Christ. Five
passages in Hebrews warn us of the danger of going back.
They are some of the most solemn words in Scripture. One
of the key words that Hebrews emphasizes, therefore, is
this word *endurance*.

And we desire that each one of you show the same diligence
to the full assurance of hope until the end, that you do not
become sluggish, but imitate those who through faith and
patience inherit the promises.

Hebrews 6:11–12

Faith and endurance. Some people will tell you that all
you need in order to claim God's promise is faith. But that
is not true. You need faith and endurance. It takes both:
"Therefore do not cast away your confidence, which has

210

great reward. For you have need of endurance, so that after you have done the will of God, you may receive the promise" (Hebrews 10:35–36).

The word *confidence* means you have freedom of speech. You can talk boldly about Jesus—about what He has done for you and what He is going to do for you. You have done the will of God, but you have not yet received the promise. What do you need? Endurance. You need to hold out from the point where you did God's will and claimed the promise to the point where you actually receive the promise. Some people do the will of God and claim the promise, but they don't hold out. Then they say it didn't work. But it will not work without endurance. You need faith and endurance.

The Tests We Will Face

What kind of testing might we face? We find the answer in Matthew 13. Jesus tells here the well-known parable of the sower who went forth with the seed. I want you to notice one little word in the verses written below: *when*. Jesus did not say *if* persecution or tribulation arises—He said *when* tribulation or persecution arises. They will arise.

In this parable Jesus speaks about the different kinds of soil, each representative of a different kind of person who hears the Word of God. Some of the seed fell by the wayside and never entered into the ground—it was caught up by the birds. Some fell on rocky ground. Some fell among thorns.

Then Jesus goes on to describe the type of person represented by each kind of soil. There is nothing profound in this; it is very simple:

"When anyone hears the word of the kingdom, and does not understand it, then the wicked one comes and snatches away what was sown in his heart. This is he who received seed by the wayside. But he who received the seed on stony

211

places, this is he who hears the word and immediately receives it with joy; yet he has no root in himself, but endures only for a while. For when tribulation or persecution arises because of the word, immediately he stumbles. Now he who received seed among the thorns is he who hears the word, and the cares of this world and the deceitfulness of riches choke the word, and he becomes unfruitful."

Matthew 13:19–22

Simply stated, there are two kinds of tests: when it is too hard and when it is too easy—the first is persecution; the second is riches. Some people cannot stand the persecution. Some people can make it when they are persecuted, but when God blesses them with riches—the beautiful home, two cars, maybe a boat—they get much more wrapped up in the things of this world than in the Kingdom of God.

There are others who receive the Word with joy. They are tremendous. They pop up the first night after they get saved and give their testimonies. Then they get baptized in the Holy Spirit, speak in tongues and prophesy. As the saying goes, they are as unquenchable in their witness as "a house afire." But three months later, you do not know where they are. Because the moment opposition and trouble came, they just wilted away. They had no root. I am almost scared when a new Christian starts too quickly. I would rather see somebody have a little struggle at the beginning.

When I worked as a pastor in London, to get one person baptized in the Holy Spirit was a victory. And I observed that for every ten persons who were baptized in the Spirit, one would stand and the rest would fall away. The opposition was so intense in those days. The people who had to struggle and fight were the ones you could rely on. The ones who had to struggle every inch of the way stood the test and stand today. So bear in mind, you are going to be tested by tribulation, and you are going to be tested by success. You have to hold out through both.

It is like running a marathon. It is not speed or strength, but endurance that counts. In Hebrews, the author envisions life in an Olympic Game setting, as a race that has to be run:

> Therefore we also, since we are surrounded by so great a cloud of witnesses, let us lay aside every weight, and the sin which so easily ensnares us, and let us run with endurance the race that is set before us.
>
> Hebrews 12:1

Remember, this is not a sprint; it is a long, deliberate race. Many people start off the Christian life as if it were a dash. A little while later they are panting beside the track; they are finished and they have hardly begun the race. But: "The race is not to the swift, nor the battle to the strong" (Ecclesiastes 9:11).

Where Paul says "lay aside every weight," we must think in terms of this race. The runner empties his pockets and wears the lightest, most flexible clothing he can. He does not carry a single unnecessary ounce of weight. We need to remember that some things are not sins, but they are weights that can burden you down and hold you back. They exhaust your strength or lure you into spending too much time and attention on them.

At the finish line, a great throng of spectators waits to see who will win. This throng of spectators is all the great saints of the Old Testament who finished their course and are waiting there ready to cheer us from the balconies of heaven.

A "Complete" Christian

The words of James urge us on:

> My brethren, count it all joy when you fall into various trials, knowing that the testing of your faith produces patience.

213

But let patience [or endurance] have its perfect work, that
you may be perfect and complete, lacking nothing.

James 1:2–4

Do you count it all joy when you fall into various trials?
Well, you need to. I need to. I need to praise God that He
counts me worthy of the trial and that He trusts me enough
to let me be tried.

Bear in mind always that the trial is for our good. James
is saying if you hold out—if you will go through the test—it
will surely shape every area of your character and personality. The test will make you a complete, fully-rounded
Christian. There will not be areas in your character that
have not been dealt with.

Do you know one of the great ways to keep a check on
your character? It is the test of close, committed fellowship—such as the small group where you meet every week
with the same people and share your life with them. After
a little while, it becomes uncomfortably clear to you that
there are some areas of your life that have never really been
dealt with. You realize that when you were not too close to
people or too intimate, you could cover up those areas. But
when you are exposed week by week to regular, intimate,
close fellowship, you either have to back out or correct your
life.

My friend Bob Mumford once said, "Suppose there are
ten areas in our character that need to be changed. You can
probably deal with six yourself. But the remaining four are
going to need other people to put their fingers on." I think
that is a pretty good average. If I do not expose myself to
others, I can deceive myself about areas of my character.
But committed fellowship does not afford me the same
opportunities to deceive myself.

Somebody once said fellowship is "roof off, walls
down." We do not mind getting the roof off because God
sees through the roof anyhow. But what about getting the

walls down and letting people see? That is harder. That takes perseverance.

This does not mean, however, that people will stay with you through the process of enduring. We see in Scripture, for instance, that Paul's support group was dwindling when he wrote his second epistle to Timothy. This was the last epistle Paul wrote, probably just shortly before his execution. "Be diligent to come to me quickly," he said, "for Demas has forsaken me, having loved this present world, and has departed for Thessalonica—Crescens for Galatia, Titus for Dalmatia. Only Luke is with me" (2 Timothy 4:9–11).

Paul had taught that the true apostle is the one who hangs on when everybody else gives up: "Truly the signs of an apostle were accomplished among you with all perseverance, in signs and wonders and mighty deeds" (2 Corinthians 12:12). The first evidence of an apostolic ministry is not miracles but perseverance.

Yet, right at the end his co-workers left him in prison. What did they lack? Endurance. What marked the apostle? Endurance. We need to ask the Lord to help us build a character of endurance.

The Temporary and the Eternal

When we seriously consider what Paul went through, we should pause before complaining about our affliction. He was beaten four times, stoned once, shipwrecked twice, left to die. He endured hunger, thirst, nakedness, peril, and yet he says:

> For our light affliction, which is but for a moment, is working for us a far more exceeding and eternal weight of glory, while we do not look at the things which are seen, but at the things which are not seen. For the things which are seen are temporary [they are not truly real, they don't last; they look glamorous, seductive, tremendous, exciting, thrilling,

but they are not permanent], but the things which are not seen are eternal.

2 Corinthians 4:17–18

Here are two principles from the Bible on how we can keep our eyes on the eternal. The first one is to make our commitment to Jesus Christ wholehearted—without any reservations. Consider the actions of Barnabas toward a group of new Christians in the city of Antioch in Syria: "When he came and had seen the grace of God, he was glad, and encouraged them all that with purpose of heart they should continue with the Lord" (Acts 11:23).

"Purpose of heart" is the key phrase. You make your mind up that you are going to stick with the Lord regardless—no matter who does or who does not. If your friends don't, you will. If your family doesn't, you will. That is purpose of heart. You are going to continue with God.

In Acts 14:22 we again find Barnabas and Paul exhorting new converts in another Antioch, Antioch in Pisidia, another city of the same name. They were "strengthening the souls of the disciples, exhorting them to continue in the faith, and saying, 'We must through many tribulations enter the kingdom of God.'"

It is hard to find another way into the Kingdom of God other than through tribulation. Keep in mind that the Word presents the Kingdom of God in two senses: the Kingdom, future, which Jesus will bring and establish, and the Kingdom that we enter into now. We live now in the Kingdom—but it is through much tribulation that we come into Kingdom living. You likely will be subjected to pressure in every area of your life. And you might say, "Why has this happened to me?" The answer is because God is preparing you for the Kingdom.

Sometimes I think we owe it to people when they come to the Lord to warn them that if they are going to move into the Kingdom, it will be through tribulation and opposition. I think it is unfair to tell new converts that when they come to

Jesus, all their problems will be solved, because it certainly rarely, if ever, will work out that way. In fact, often you will have problems you never knew existed before.

The second principle of keeping our eyes on the eternal comes from one of my favorite passages of Scripture: Hebrews 11:27. Moses grew up in Egypt and was destined to inherit the throne as the son of Pharaoh's daughter. He had everything that the world could offer—education, wealth, social privilege. At the age of forty he turned his back on it, fled from Egypt and spent the next forty years looking after a few sheep in the back side of the desert. What a test of character! "By faith [Moses] forsook Egypt, not fearing the wrath of the king; for he endured as seeing Him who is invisible" (Hebrews 11:27).

In this one short verse we discover the essence of endurance: seeing Him who is invisible. How do you see that which is invisible? What faculty enables you to see it? The answer is faith. Faith is related to the unseen. Faith is a sure conviction concerning things not seen. If you and I are going to hold out, the unseen world has got to be more real to us than the seen.

Paul put it like this:

> Now the Lord is the Spirit; and where the Spirit of the Lord is, there is liberty. But we all, with unveiled face, beholding as in a mirror the glory of the Lord, are being transformed into the same image from glory to glory, just as by the Spirit of the Lord.
>
> 2 Corinthians 3:17–18

The "mirror" is the Word of God and it shows us the invisible. The Bible says that while we look in this mirror, the Holy Spirit reveals to us the glory of the Lord, and we are changed into the likeness of what we see. The more we look in it, the more effectively the Holy Spirit can work in us, building our character through persecution and tribulation.

27

Finishing the Course

Webster's *New World Dictionary* defines *endurance* as "fortitude" and "the ability to last, continue, or remain." We are indeed learning both the cost and the blessing connected to the ability to remain.

Many years ago in London, the daughter of a Swedish pastor lived with us for about three months learning English, which I taught her. She was a beautiful, talented girl with a lovely singing voice. Her father was the pastor of the largest Pentecostal church in Sweden, and she had grown up in a strict Pentecostal environment.

When this girl was about fourteen years old, she was listening to what all her friends at school talked about—all the pleasures of the theater and dancing and things like that. And she became more and more interested. So one day she went to her father and said, "Father, I want to thank you for the care that you've given me, the way you trained me and brought me up. But I want to tell you that from now on I want to go another way. I want to find out what the world has to offer. I hear all my friends talking about it, and I want to find out for myself."

And her father, who was a wise man, said, "Barbara, your mother and I will pray for you." He did not argue. He did not say it was wrong. He said, "We'll pray."

That night, the daughter had the most vivid dream of her life. In this dream she saw two cities. One was a big, modern, beautiful city. It was filled with lights flashing and glittering everywhere. Across a valley was another city that had a different kind of light. It did not flash, it did not glitter; it was steady and calm. While she was looking at the beautiful city with the glittering neon lights, a man introduced himself to her. He was very cultured, very educated and very well dressed. He said, "I'd like to show you around this city." And she went with him.

The further she went with him, the uglier he became. Soon she realized it was the devil himself. As she stopped there in horror, all the lights in this neon city began to go out one by one by one until the city was in total darkness. She turned to look across at the other city, and it was as bright and clear as it had always been. The next day she went to her father and said, "Daddy, I'm coming to church with you." She was a wise girl. She listened when the Lord spoke.

Often when Lydia and I were in a big, modern city and we would see all those neon lights and the traffic and the excitement, the exhilaration and the pleasure, we would turn to one another and say, "Do you remember Barbara's dream?" One night all those lights will go out. That is coming very soon. All those lights are going out.

Let me quote Paul again:

> For our light affliction, which is but for a moment, is working for us a far more exceeding and eternal weight of glory, while we do not look at the things which are seen, but at the things which are not seen.
>
> 2 Corinthians 4:17–18

Those are the things that are eternal. They do not change. They are in the Word.

Stay in the Word. Don't take just five minutes a day with your Bible. Read it. Meditate on it. Believe it. Live in it. Ask the Holy Spirit to make it real to you. And that Word will become so real to you that there will be nothing in this world that could tempt you or attract you in any disloyalty to Jesus Christ.

I believe in enjoying life—in exercise and in pleasure. I have been delivered from legalism—in which I spent many years—but I do not want to love the world nor the things that are in the world. Because "If anyone loves the world, the love of the Father is not in him" (1 John 2:15). And I owe everything to my Father. I don't want to be disloyal to Him. I want to show Him my gratitude and appreciation. He has made me His child and an heir of Christ, and I want to show Him I appreciate His goodness. I want to keep my eyes on the things that are not seen.

I am a realist and live a practical life. I believe in having things in order. I answer my letters and pay my bills. Both of my feet are on the ground, but my eyes are on the unseen. There is such a thin veil between us and eternity. A simple, old song says, "Sometimes I grow homesick for heaven." Well, I really do. And yet, I am not complaining about earth. God has treated me better than I could have ever hoped or deserved. But never forget that there is something beyond time.

Another old song says, "I have decided to follow Jesus. . . . Tho' none go with me, still I will follow. . . . The past behind me, the cross before me—No turning back, no turning back!" The first time I ever heard that chorus was a November night in 1947 in the city of Jerusalem. My wife and I and our eight daughters had just fled our home under cover of night and taken refuge in an American mission in the center of Jerusalem. We were without food, without a home, without anything. We had walked out in the middle of the night and left everything. When I got to that mission, they were singing that song. It was the first time I had ever heard it, "Tho' none go with me, still I will follow."

I have two more endurance-builders to share with you. The first one is as important as it is simple: When you fail, don't give up. Others have failed before you—and I am one of them. One of the devil's cleverest tricks is to convince you that you are a failure and that you might as well give up. He will try to tell you that God has given up on you. Don't believe him. He is a liar. The Word says: "The steps of a good man are ordered by the Lord, and He delights in his way. Though he fall, he shall not be utterly cast down; for the Lord upholds him with His hand" (Psalm 37:23–24).

Have you ever fallen? Remember that you will not be utterly cast down because the Lord still has your hand. We have noted an amazing Old Testament example of this fact in the life of King David. He fell terribly, tragically. And yet God forgave him and restored him. David was able to say, "Even when you fall, don't give up. God will pick you up."

There is also a New Testament example of a man who fell and learned that the Lord had never let go of him. His name was Peter. Jesus spoke these two verses to Peter, knowing that Peter was going to deny Him three times: "And the Lord said, 'Simon, Simon! Indeed, Satan has asked for you, that he may sift you as wheat. But I have prayed for you, that your faith should not fail'" (Luke 22:31–32).

What a depth in those verses! Jesus did not pray that Peter would not deny Him, He prayed that his faith would not fail. If Peter's faith had failed, there would have been no way back. So when you fall, stretch out your hand and let the Lord pick you up. And don't give up—because He has not given up on you.

Finally, remember the prize giving. Not all the issues of life are settled in the here and now. There are some that remain for the future. Look at the words of Paul written from jail to Timothy: "I have fought the good fight, I have finished the race, I have kept the faith" (2 Timothy 4:7).

Those three achievements go together. If you are going to keep the faith, you have to fight the fight. Faith is a fight. You cannot escape the fight and keep the faith. If you are going to finish your course, you have got to fight the fight. Paul said, "I've done all three. I've finished the race. I've fought the fight. I've kept the faith." Then he said, "From now on I'm waiting for the prize giving." Look at verse 8: "There is laid up for me the crown of righteousness, which the Lord, the righteous Judge, will give to me on that Day."

Paul had been condemned to execution by an unjust, unrighteous ruler—the emperor Nero. There had been no justice in his trial, but he said that that was not the last word. He said there is going to be another judgment day: "There is going to be prize giving. And the judge will be absolutely just. It will be the Lord Himself, and He will give me my prize—my victor's crown."

For many years of my life, prize giving was an important part of my school days. And I won many prizes. But there is one prize that still has to be won, and that is only for those who keep the faith, fight the fight and finish the course. I believe that Paul was true to the end because he saw something beyond time. He looked out into eternity, and he saw the great prize-giving when the gold, silver and bronze medals will be given out. And I think some of us will be rather surprised at who gets the gold medals. It will not be the speed with which we ran. It will be the faithfulness with which we served. The Lord's emphasis is on faithfulness. Remember Jesus' words: "Well done, good and faithful servant" (Matthew 25:23).

For many of us, the days that lie ahead are days that are going to test our endurance. They are not going to be easy. The persecution we endure is going to test one thing above all others: our loyalty—both to the Lord and to the

Body of Christ. I want to be able to look at my brothers and sisters and say, "I've kept the faith. I haven't been disloyal. I haven't betrayed you."

I really believe that is the test that lies ahead of us: the test of character and loyalty—the test of how well we let ourselves be trained by the Holy Spirit—the test of faithfulness in spiritual battle.

If you will finish the course, glory to God, you will have engaged in battle—and won.

Derek Prince (1915–2003) was born in India of British parents. He was educated as a scholar of Greek and Latin at Eton College and Cambridge University, England, where he held a fellowship in ancient and modern philosophy at King's College. He also studied several modern languages, including Hebrew and Aramaic, at Cambridge University and the Hebrew University in Jerusalem.

While serving with the British Army in World War II, Derek began to study the Bible and experienced a life-changing encounter with Jesus Christ. Out of that encounter he formed two conclusions: first, that Jesus Christ is alive; and second, that the Bible is a true, relevant, up-to-date book. These conclusions altered the course of his life, which he then devoted to studying and teaching the Bible.

Derek's main gift of explaining the Bible and its teaching in a clear, simple way has helped build a foundation of faith in millions of lives. His nondenominational, nonsectarian approach makes his teaching relevant and helpful to people from all racial and religious backgrounds.

He is the author of more than 50 books and his teaching is featured on 500 audio and 160 video teaching cassettes, many of which have been translated and published in more than 60 languages. His daily radio broadcast, *Derek Prince Legacy Radio*, is translated into Arabic, Chinese (Amoy, Cantonese, Mandarin, Shanghaiese, Swatow), Croatian, German, Malagasy, Mongolian, Russian, Samoan, Spanish and Tongan. The program continues to touch lives around the world.

For more information on Derek Prince and the many teaching resources available, please contact:

Derek Prince Ministries
P.O. Box 19501
Charlotte, NC 28219-9501
(704) 357-3556
www.derekprince.org